*Act Like*

*a Success,*

*Think Like*

*a Success*

# *Act Like a Success,*

# Think Like a Success

## DISCOVERING YOUR GIFT
## AND THE WAY TO LIFE'S RICHES

# STEVE HARVEY

### with Jeffrey Johnson

## Amistad
*An Imprint of HarperCollinsPublishers*

HarperCollins books may be purchased for educational, business, or sales promotional use. For information, please e-mail
the Special Markets Department at SPsales@harpercollins.com.

A hardcover edition of this book was published in 2014 by
Amistad, an imprint of HarperCollins Publishers.

FIRST AMISTAD PAPERBACK EDITION PUBLISHED 2015

Library of Congress Cataloging-in-Publication Data has been
applied for.

ISBN: 978-0-06-222033-2 (pbk.)

17  18  19   OV/RRD   10 9 8 7 6 5 4

To my beloved mother, Eloise Vera Harvey, who was a devoted Sunday school teacher for forty years. She blessed my heart and soul with the gift of faith. My faith has been the cornerstone of my existence and of everything I have overcome and of everything that I am, and for that I love her so, and I miss her ever more every day.

To my father, whose sole job was to teach me manhood, and that he did, and he imbued me with an incredible work ethic, for which I owe him my entire career. Thank you, father.

To Marjorie, my wife, who came along and allowed for everything that my parents instilled in me to rise to the top. She has been an inspiration, a motivation. She is the love of my life. She is much of the reason I am who I am. I love you, girl!

# CONTENTS

*Introduction:*

Your Gift Is Calling . . .

Are You Ready to Answer?

1

# CONTENTS

# Act Like

## a Success,

### Think Like

#### a Success

# Your Gift Is Calling . . .
# Are You Ready to Answer?

There I was riding on a private jet with Cedric "the Entertainer." We were being flown from the set of *The Steve Harvey Show* to a city where we were going to perform as the Kings of Comedy—when it was just me, Bernie Mac, and Ced. Everybody in the passenger cabin on the jet was asleep. When I looked out the window, I could see the lights sparkling in the city below. Next thing I knew, tears were streaming down my face.

At that point, I hadn't taken full inventory of my life and all of my blessings and achievements. I couldn't believe that I was sitting on a G3 jet that was sent by the tour promoters. I thought, Look at what my life has become. I had been told that I would never amount to anything. But I had made it through the miserable carpet-cleaning business; selling insurance, which I didn't enjoy; the weeks on the road with no gigs; quitting my job; homelessness; and getting laid off. I realized that I had been through a lot.

Suddenly, an overwhelming sense of accomplishment flooded over me and the tears continued to flow. It hit me that my dreams were coming true. I had wanted to be one of the premier comedians in the country, and it was happening. The announcement of the tour gave us a title—the Kings of Comedy—and then we came out and proved it to be true. We became the largest-grossing comedy routine of all time. The tour took in $58 million! My dreams were coming true right in front of me. That was the first moment, on that jet, that I recall feeling success—really feeling the joy, contentment, and true alignment with God's purpose for me.

Success for me is not about the car I drive, the house I live in, the way I travel, or the suits I wear. Part of my success is connected to the money I earn and the things I am able to do for my family and myself. But anyone who knows me well will tell you that money is the smallest part of my success. Success is being in the marriage of my dreams with a woman who helps me be my best. Success is expressing my love for my children and having the opportunity to work with them as I build and expand my business. Success is working my butt off every day doing what I love to do.

Your definition of success may be slightly different, but we tend to desire the same things in life—peace of mind, loving friends and family, good health, and a certain level of financial comfort. Whatever your definition of success, this life-changing book will put you on the right track to achieving it.

Spending your hard-earned dollars to purchase *Act Like a Success, Think Like a Success* is an indication that you are serious about taking your life to a new level and attaining all that the world has to offer you. And this book will not let you down in helping you get there. I have written these pages with many people in mind—whether you are a college student, a recent graduate trying to find your way in the work world, a retiree seeking what comes next, or someone who is on top and trying to stay there. It's for you if you are just starting out, or have decided to stop struggling with obstacles that you are determined to overcome, or have already been climbing the mountain and can't find the motivation to climb anymore. It's for those of you who have fallen. It's for those of you who have traveled part of the way and discovered that this can't be all the world has to offer you.

My first book, *Act Like a Lady, Think Like a Man*, helped millions of women take a fresh look at their relationships and dating behavior. *Act Like a Success, Think Like a Success* will help you to evaluate your life goals and determine the means to achieving them. My previous books targeted women as the primary audience. *Act Like a Success, Think Like a Success* was created to empower everyone—men and women, young and old, fresh to the workforce or newly retired. This book is enriched with compelling material that can help no matter where you are on your journey.

*Act Like a Success, Think Like a Success* lets you know that it is not good enough to simply exist. Life is more than wading through a lifeless job, earning a gold watch, and cashing in your 401(k). Your life has to be more than just waiting for the right opportunity to come along and find you. Your life has to be more than just marking time watching others achieve success. The words in this book will motivate you to get the most out of your life by using something that you already have—your gift.

My gift is making people laugh. You have a very special gift, too. Our creator, in his infinite wisdom, created every single soul with a gift. Your gift may be totally unique or it may be similar to someone else's, but know that your gift is *yours*.

When we utilize our gift, the universe thanks us by giving us an abundance of riches—from abundant opportunities to good health to financial wealth. When you aren't sowing into the soil of the universe, you notice that things in your life just seem to dry up and get worse. But when you sow back into the universe with your time, your passion, and your commitment to others, the world will offer abundant opportunities for you to blossom into the new you. Incorporating your gift into your life and sharing it with others will bring you joy, passion, and a new vigor for living life to the fullest. This book will show you how to manifest your gift in your life.

This book also focuses on how you can transfer your gift to other important areas in your life, such as building a better working relationship with your boss or investing more in your community or strengthening your family. *Act Like a Success, Think Like a Success* will get you thinking about increasing your life in whole new ways.

The success I'm enjoying now didn't just happen overnight. I had to learn to be successful, and the life I have now is literally a dream come true. *Act Like a Success, Think Like a Success* is full of information about what I have learned on my journey to self-fulfillment. I want to share it with you so that you, too, can see your dreams made real in your life.

## HOW TO GET THE MOST OUT OF THIS BOOK

Part One of *Act Like a Success, Think Like a Success* deals with being real about where you are right now. We are going to get brutally honest about overcoming your fears, releasing your limitations, and taking the lid off of life.

Part Two focuses on helping you to determine your gift. Once you know what your gift is, I offer tips on attaching it to just the right vehicle for transforming your life. You will be doing what you love. When you exercise this opportunity, you will see great changes in your life. The initial change will occur within you. You will exude a radiance that will serve as a magnet, drawing closer to you other success-minded people with similar drive and ambition. You will enter into a realm of successful thinking. I discuss creating a vision board to serve as a regular reminder to stay on course in your travels to a bigger life.

After you have attached your gift to a vehicle, you will need to sharpen your professional makeup to allow your gift to work best for you.

Part Three reveals ways to enhance your gift. These chapters present valuable information and tools for accentuating and utilizing your skill set. They include advice on goal setting and its relation to making your dreams come true. These practical suggestions are something you can implement in your life immediately. Learning how to walk in your gift doesn't make life perfect, but it gives your life purpose and meaning.

I remind you that being able to self-evaluate your performance with honesty is a major key to success. This section talks about the value of time. I cover the necessity of saying no and of asking for what you want, as well as of dealing with self-doubt. I also address the concept of "everyone who comes with you cannot go with you."

*Act Like a Success, Think Like a Success* closes with inspiring words to encourage you to share your wealth. This section capitalizes on three important themes: healing yourself from haters with success, learning the keys to having a balanced life, and allowing your blessings to bless someone else.

*Act Like a Success, Think Like a Success* is not meant for you to simply read and walk away unchanged. It engages you with Success Actions: In these spaces, I encourage you to write down your reflections, aspirations, and visions for your life. When initiated, this will serve as your Success Action Plan. Be accountable for what you create as you uncover your gifts and talents.

Establish a team if you need help staying motivated and

applying the tools for success. Together, your team should read the book, share notes, and assess goals. This will provide the support you may need to reach your next level of success.

I have also created an online community of people just like you who are committed to *Act Like a Success, Think Like a Success*, at www.actlikeasuccess.com. You can join with people all over the world who are working to increase their life. You can use this website to develop your own Success Plan. The website includes an area where you can track your thinking and action changes, receive inspirational messages from some of the most incredible people on the planet, and even leave your own testimonies about your growth.

If you're on Twitter or Instagram, you can send me a tweet or video about your progress to @ActLikeASuccess, using the hashtag #IAmSuccess.

Many self-help and inspirational books tell you that you need to get something that you don't already have in order to achieve greatness. I'm here to tell you that you don't have to take another class, learn another language, get with a new set of people, or spend money you don't have. To become truly successful in your life, you have to start with your *gift*. And you know what's so great about that? You already have it! I know that some of you do not yet know what your gift is. Others of you may have an idea of what your gift is, but you haven't figured out how to appreciate it, perfect it, and attach it to the right vehicle that will lead you to even more success than you can ever imagine. You have all the answers right here in these pages.

In my journey toward success, I came to realize that *staying* successful is as much an art as *becoming* successful. When you really take on acting like a success and thinking like a success, you can have all the riches that life has to offer. This is the kind of blessed life that I want you to start living.

# PART ONE

# *When Enough Is Enough*

# CHAPTER 1

## "I'm Tired of Myself"

I speak on being tired of myself rather well because the Steve Harvey that you know was once tired of himself at a particular point in his life. I, Steve Harvey, was tired. I was tired of the way I was living. I was tired of going nowhere. I was sick and tired of being poor. Poverty had exhausted me. It was exhausting for me to constantly have to think up ways to provide and survive. It was difficult to see things that I wanted and not be able to afford them. I was completely worn out by poverty. I was sick of myself for not pursuing my God-given gift. I was tired of myself for not going after my dreams.

At that time, I did not really know how to pursue my

dreams, but still, that is not an excuse, because not know-ing did not stop the sickening feeling I was having. I was tired of struggling, of doing without. I was tired of me. I was tired of everything. I was tired of feeling disappoint-ment. I was tired of disappointing other people, including my mother and father. I was tired of not being able to see the potential in myself that others clearly saw. I was tired of living in a rut.

I had gotten completely and fully tired of myself. I was exhausted from looking outside myself for the answers. But I came to realize that the solution to my pain and despair were deep inside of me all along. As my mother used to say, paraphrasing Fannie Lou Hamer, "Sometimes, son, noth-ing is going to change until you get sick and tired of being sick and tired."

Let's take this journey together, because if you are tired of being sick and tired, know this: so was I.

## ARE YOU TIRED OF YOURSELF?

Are you tired of making the same promises to yourself that you are never motivated enough to see through? Are you tired of making excuses for not making change? Are you tired of measuring yourself against others and falling short? Are you sick of telling yourself, "Tomorrow I will do something different," but that "tomorrow" never comes? Well, being tired of yourself is a good place to be, because it means that you are ready to make changes in your life that will bring about great reward. I'm glad that you're finally here.

When you are in this position of being tired of yourself, normally you are not alone. Everybody in your life—from your family to your coworkers—has been tired of you and your excuses for some time now. They see your gift and the pain you are causing yourself by not tapping into your God-given purpose and becoming your best. But here's the thing: People can tell you that they are tired of your excuses, but until *you* get tired of you, it won't make any difference. Are you done with blocking yourself from opportunities that could easily have been yours last month, last year, or even a decade ago?

More often than not, our beliefs about ourselves are learned, internalized thoughts that evolve into behaviors that take over how we operate in our day-to-day lives. Somewhere along the way we grow accustomed to our self-perceptions, and we allow them to become oppositions to our gifts and opportunities. We become our own opposition when we accept the following: procrastinating, lying to ourselves, comparing ourselves to others, and having self-doubts—in short, anything that gets in the way of our becoming who we were created to be.

So, what does it take for you to get to the breaking point? What will it take for you to be awakened out of your sleep? What will force you to realize finally that the life you are living is far below your God-given potential? This is your life, and you have to live it TODAY. You cannot afford to waste another minute being unfulfilled, unsatisfied, and underutilized. Right now, and I do mean *right now*, is your moment to take advantage of the dreams, goals, and visions that you have held in your heart for far too long.

Jordan Belfort, the author of the book and inspiration for the movie *The Wolf of Wall Street*, said, "The only thing standing between you and your goal is the bullshit story you keep telling yourself as to why you can't achieve it." But I want to take it a step further. Excuses are the lies you convince yourself are true to avoid proving you are worthy of the gift you were given. Say this with me—"NO MORE EXCUSES."

When I was a student at Kent State University, my major was psychology, but I was really majoring in excuses. I had a million excuses for why I couldn't go to class or why I couldn't pay my rent. After college, I had even more excuses for why I was stuck in dead-end jobs and why I wasn't pursuing my dream to be a comedian. The more I told myself these lies, the more I believed that I wasn't worthy of earning my degree or being on a comedy stage.

Then one day I was telling a friend why I had dropped out of school, and when I heard the words coming out of my mouth, I realized that it wasn't the school's fault or my parents' fault. At the end of the day, it was *my* fault. I had everything I needed, but at every turn I found a reason not to start. I came up with roadblocks for myself so that I wouldn't have to be responsible for my gift.

If you are like I was, you need to stop lying to yourself with excuses. Your excuses are as empty now as they were when you first started using them. I need you to realize that your gifts are opportunities, and to embrace a new belief: *You* are a success.

Now, before you skip this section and say, "Steve, I don't make excuses for my life," hold on. The people who claim that they don't make excuses are usually the biggest offenders. You know who you are. You are a Type A person who goes hard in your career, but you are normally the one making an excuse for missing a family member's birthday or canceling a date for the third time. Success doesn't live in one part of your life and become exempt in another. If you're going to do this, you have to do it all the way. You have to be open to using your gift to embrace your opportunities and change your life.

When I began in comedy, I was protective about letting people into my life. I was trying to write like other people. I didn't really develop the real truth of who I was as a stand-up until I was no longer afraid to open up. Sharing my truth led me to tons more material to joke about, including my past, my relationship with my parents, my failed relationships, and things I was currently going through. For me to grow in my gift, the first thing I had to do was to learn to be honest.

When you open up yourself to being honest, you can just deal with whatever the truth is. All of your truth may be negative, but that can be a positive, too. If you uncover the negatives about yourself, you then have a chance to improve. That's why it's very important that when something goes wrong in your relationship, or when something goes wrong in your business, the first question you ask yourself is "What did I do wrong?" You have an opportunity to change yourself or fix the situation at any given moment. You cannot change another person. If I point the one finger at everyone else and ignore the three pointing back at me, I have relinquished my chance to grow, change, and develop. But the moment that I pay attention to the three fingers that are pointing back at me, then and only then will I grow.

Too often you focus on the cons before you even consider a pro. You can't even think about the benefits of taking on your dream because you're too busy focusing on the "what if," the "what could be," and the "why it won't work for me" excuses. You're willing to waste years of your life walking away from your dreams instead of running toward your destiny.

## THE COMPARISON CURSE

Some of you are afraid to step up into your gifts because you're too busy comparing yourself to someone else. God made you and the way you do what you do *exclusively* for you. The world doesn't have time to interact with your representative—it needs the real, *authentic* you to show up and shine your light.

Don't get stuck thinking, Well, there's already a million and one motivational speakers out there. There's nothing new that I can bring to the table. There might be fifty motivational speakers in your city, but you are the only one who has your unique set of experiences, mistakes, lessons, pitfalls, and triumphs that can make the difference between someone living an ordinary life and that same person stepping into an extraordinary future. You'd be amazed how your personal story about leaving your small town and taking a leap of faith in the big city could speak to someone louder than, say, a story told by Les Brown ever could. Use your energy to perfect your game, not someone else's.

## "I'M NOT READY TO SIT AT THE BIG TABLE"

Often, we get these stereotypes stuck in our heads about who can and who can't sit at the Big Table to make decisions. We count ourselves out before the game starts because we think we don't have the right upbringing, education, or experience to take on a new opportunity.

When the day comes for you to be part of a meeting that will change the course of your organization, you can't afford to back away from the table because you think you don't have enough letters behind your name.

I don't care about your race, your gender, where you come from, or your financial status. If God gives you the opportunity to step up to the plate, don't waste your time talking about "I'm not worthy"! Stop limiting your gift because you can't see the big picture. You have the same right to sit at the Big Table as anyone else. For far too long, the Big Tables have been dominated by the same kinds of people and personalities. Sit up, speak with boldness about what you know, and add value that would be absent from the table if you remained silent. Take your opportunity to add your unique talents and skills to the mix.

We have to be aware of the conversation we are having with ourselves about our gifts and talents. What are you saying to yourself when no one else is around? What are the conversations that you are having in the mirror with yourself each morning? Are you speaking life into your dreams, or are you repeating someone else's fears and anxieties? Are you front-loading your day with Scriptures, affirmations, and positive quotations, or are you dumping doubt and anguish into your spirit?

Some of us have been playing the same self-defeating records over and over again in our heads for so long that we don't know how to think any differently about ourselves.

"I'm not smart enough to do that."

"I'll never be as good as my mother [or father]."

"That's good for you, but I know that won't work for somebody like me."

"It's too hard to do that."

"It's too late for me to get out there and do it."

You may be thinking that you're just having these self-defeating conversations with yourself, but the more you repeat these statements in your head, the more these words become like an invisible coat of misery that you put on every day. You think that you're the only one who can see your words of defeat, but they show up in your demeanor and how you present yourself to the world.

How do you get a new song to sing about for your life and your dreams? You can start out small, by saying short affirmations:

"I was BORN to do this!"

"God has a plan for ME!"

"I am MORE than a conqueror!"

"My dreams CAN become my reality!"

## GET FLUENT IN THE LANGUAGE OF SUCCESS

Practice learning how to speak about success with experts who are fluent in the language of success. One of the best ways to learn a foreign language is to fully immerse yourself into the culture of the people who speak the language best. The same principle applies to speaking the language of success. You want to be around people who know how to speak million-dollar deals into existence. You want to be in a conversation when the next great nonprofit is born. You want your ears to be accustomed to listening for the next great idea that is going to revolutionize the world.

Imagine, what could you really accomplish if your speech was filled with more statements that began with "I can" than with "I can't"? How far could your dreams soar if you said, "Why not me?" instead of "Why me?" more often? And just like when you are learning a new language, you're still going to slip up and say, "I could have done . . ." instead of "I will do . . ." Surround yourself with native successful speakers, and before you know it, you'll begin to speak the life of your dreams into existence.

Some parts of your vision are meant to be shared, in confidence, only with a trusted mentor, friend, or family member. And some aspects of your vision honestly don't need to go beyond your prayer time with God.

## YOU GOTTA PUT YOUR NAME ON THE LEASE

So many people are missing their way in life because they are afraid to sign the lease on their gift. You can clearly see your dream, but you are wasting time overthinking the unknown or talking to people who don't understand your aspirations. I know far too many people in Hollywood who go around saying, "I'm a waitress for now, but I'm really an actress." Then why aren't you acting already? If you are committed to making your dream a reality, you gotta put your name on the lease.

You will miss out on the true blessing of your life if you don't accept that your gift is your winning ticket and the key to your life's blessings.

All you have to do is commit to your gift. Once you commit, the rest of it—the money, the connections, and the opportunities—will start coming to you in ways that you can't imagine. Let me put it another way: When you put your efforts into your gift, you are giving God something to bless. I never expected to fail at comedy. I only expected to succeed. Even when I faced some of my darkest times, I would just hold on to those little pieces of light along the way until those lights turned into an open field of opportunity.

## Success Actions

I want you to take a few minutes and think about all the excuses you've made in the last week. Write them all down on the next page. Now, circle or highlight the ones that you use the most. We're going to call these your Top 3 Excuses. Write these down on page 27. Below your Top 3 Excuses, write down three expectations to replace these excuses. We will name these your Top 3 Expectations.

Need help defining the two? Here are my definitions:

**Excuses**       **Why I can't**
**Expectations**  **Why I will**

See the difference? Excuses are self-imposed roadblocks, detours, and traffic jams that take you off your road to success. Expectations are wide-open lanes reserved for those people who are willing to pay the price for excellence.

What are the new expectations that you can create for your life? What will you begin to tell yourself when life gets hard? You got them? Now write them down.

My Favorite Excuses

- LATER.

_____

_____

_____

_____

_____

_____

_____

_____

_____

_____

_____

_____

Top 3 Excuses

1. _____

_____

_____

2. _____

_____

_____

3. _____

_____

_____


Top 3 Expectations

1. _____

_____

_____

2. _____

_____

_____

3. _____

_____

_____

If you're serious about this, I want you to take your new expectations one step further by writing them on a clean sheet of paper and signing it. These new declarations will be your commitment to yourself, marking the beginning of your journey to greatness.

# CHAPTER 2

# Fear and Failure

During one of my early appearances on Bishop T. D. Jakes's talk show, I made a bold proclamation: "I am the most fearless person you will ever meet." I don't know what made me say it, because I had never said something like that before in my life. I figured that the bishop and his team really liked what I had to say because they used that sound bite in the video promos advertising my appearance on the show.

But here's the real deal: I am afraid a lot. I was afraid to pursue my talk show because I thought it might not work out. I was afraid to do syndicated radio because I didn't know if I would be accepted in enough markets to be successful. I was afraid to take on the Kings of Comedy tour. When Walter Latham came to us and said, "We are going to be playing in basketball arenas," I was scared. The largest crowd I had ever performed in front of at that point was five thousand people—and that was on a good night. When I interviewed President Obama, I was terrified because I didn't want to blow it. Before I did Bishop Jakes's Mega-Fest, I tossed and turned for three nights in a row.

My biggest moment of fear came when I did my first one-hour HBO special. I had never been more afraid of anything in my entire career. The Bell Auditorium in Augusta, Georgia, was completely sold out, and I was positioned backstage behind a sheer curtain, waiting for the show to start. My heart was beating so hard that I could literally see the pocket square in my suit rising and falling. If you look closely at the footage from that special, you can even see my hands glistening with sweat.

Something went wrong with the timing for opening up the main curtains to begin the show. And I was anxious as I waited behind the curtain for a good six to seven minutes. But even though I was out of the audience's view, I could just feel their love saying, "Come on, Steve. Do not let us down."

When the curtain finally rose, the crowd went crazy. I grabbed the mike and just let it swing for a minute in order to collect my cool. When I finally started talking, I heard my voice begin to quiver. I just kept praying, "Lord, please calm me down. Come on, Lord. This is my only HBO special. Please, God." And guess what? About fifteen minutes into my set, all my nerves disappeared and I was hot as smoke. That set became one of my best specials to date.

What I learned from that moment is that when you face your fears, they aren't as big as you thought they were. What makes them big is when you don't turn around to face them head-on. The longer you avoid your fears, the bigger they grow in your mind. As I stood behind that malfunctioning curtain, I kept thinking, Lord Jesus, look at all these people. The longer I stood there, the more I realized that I could keep worrying about the twenty-four hundred people in the room and fail, or I could just go out there . . . and I could actually win. It really just comes down to deciding whether you want to win or lose.

## FAILURE IS PART OF THE PROCESS

Most people fail because they become paralyzed by their fear. You have to choose: "Am I going to face my fears and go see what my life can *really* be?" or "Am I going to suc-

cumb to my fears and do exactly what I've always done"?
When you go with the latter, you've set yourself up for
failure yet again because you didn't even attempt to win.
How many times do we allow ourselves to avoid getting
things done in our lives simply because we fear what we
think the outcome is going to be?

I have taught myself just to go try something if there
is even a remote possibility of something great happening
for my life and my career. You have to learn to convince
yourself that the possibility is greater than the inevitability
of doing nothing. Listen, if you are an entrepreneur who
is passionate about your product, but you never ask anyone
to buy what you are selling, it will never get sold. Sure,
there's a possibility that you can deliver your best sales pitch
in your best Sunday suit and they will still say no. But so
what? Do you know how many times I've been told no for
movie scripts, television shows, and comedy specials? A
whole hell of lot more times than I heard yes.

You know how many jokes I've written that nobody
has laughed at? Thousands. I have a whole cemetery full of
dead jokes with tombstones standing above them.

But in all seriousness, I took those bad jokes out of my
act and I learned how to get good at my craft. There are
many jokes that I wish I had never written, and there are
some that I have knocked out the park. But guess what? I

now have six comedy specials with eight hours of original, A-list jokes, and in them I never repeated a single one.

You want to hear something shocking? Eighty-five percent of small businesses in this country fail within the first two years. Eight-five percent! That's a whole lot of failure.

Warren Buffett said that he would not invest in any business where the owner hasn't failed at least twice. I love that truly wealthy and successful people understand that failure is part of the process.

But far too often when we face the failure of a business venture, we let that failure paralyze us from trying again. The failure could stem from a lack of financial planning, a lack of resources, or the lack of the right team members. But you have to realize that failure is part of the process when you are on the road to success.

The only way to get back on track is to come up with another plan. I've failed more times than I can count. But you can't let the failure freeze you in place and stop you from pursuing your dreams.

## THE BOMB IN CHARLOTTE

When I was doing stand-up comedy full-time, I quickly learned that the hardest night is not your first one; it's that night when you have to go back out there after you've had a really bad one. I had an experience like that during the first night of the original Kings of Comedy tour in Charlotte, North Carolina. My mother had just died, and my mind just wasn't there. In addition, I had just finished a live comedy special, but I was so messed up that I didn't even watch it.

Each of us Kings was supposed to do a thirty-minute set, but Ced got up there and did forty-seven minutes. Bernie's set got so good that he stayed up there for a whole hour! They were ripping the room so much that the arena had to call a mandatory break. Then there was a malfunction with a piece of equipment, and the break ended up lasting forty-five minutes.

So here I come, trying to deliver my set after these people had already sat through almost two hours of comedy between Ced and Bernie plus an unanticipated forty-five-minute break. When I walked out there, it was horrific. I was doing jokes from my comedy special. I didn't realize that most of the people there had already heard them. People were booing, arguing, and fussing, and I just became discombobulated. All I can say is that it was a rough night.

On the way to the airport the next morning, a Charlotte deejay named A.J. let into me. He said, "Ced and Bernie were hot, but Steve is no King of Comedy." He predicted that the tour was going to be a complete disaster. I knew this guy personally, and I was miffed that he was playing me so cold. By the time we got to the airport, I ran into a few people who'd seen my performance the night before, and they were trying to be encouraging by saying, "Steve, it's all right. We love you anyway." I appreciated their support.

Once we boarded the plane and got settled, I started writing. When we landed in Kansas City later that day, I shut myself up in my hotel room, and I wrote, and wrote, and wrote some more. Before I knew it, I had written a brand-new, forty-five-minute set. I got so lost in writing, revising, and practicing in the mirror that when Bernie came up to my room to grab me for dinner, I said, "Nah, I'm just going to stay here and finish working on this."

The next night in Kansas City, I had a long talk with Bernie and Ced, and I told them that they had to stick closer to a thirty-minute set. But Ced went out there and did forty minutes, and Bernie followed up with forty-eight. So much for them following the time limit. There was a twenty-minute intermission after Bernie, and I started to get scared, because I had bombed so badly in Charlotte.

When I finally got up there, I killed it. I left the stage that night and every night for the next two years with a standing ovation.

Our first two nights in Charlotte and Kansas City helped me to begin looking at failure differently. I learned that failure doesn't have to be this life-shattering, I'm-never-going-to-do-this-again experience but is in fact an opportunity to gain a valuable learning experience. I knew Kansas City was going to be a hard night to get through at first, but if I hadn't gone through such an awful night in Charlotte, I would never have written that new forty-five-minute set. My failure in Charlotte gave me the right experience that I needed to rip up the stage the next night in Kansas City.

Many times when people graduate from college, they can barely get a job. Why? Because they don't have experience. No employer wants to hire someone who has never lost before, who has never failed before, or who has never made a mistake before. Employers want someone who is experienced with failure, has learned from it, and can get the job done. So, you see, failure is not here to defeat you, but to give you the power to gain those life experiences that you can come back to and learn from again and again.

## OPENING THE DOORS OF YOUR PERSONAL PRISONS

I've learned to seek wisdom from people from all walks of life, including men and women in the prison system. Many people look at prisoners as failures. The reality is that they failed to do right and were caught. But the fact that they are incarcerated does not mean they are failures at everything. It depends on their response to their predicament. They may have limitations on their freedom, but I love it when prisoners determine that the prison system can't own their souls. They have found peace with the actions that landed them behind bars; they've asked for forgiveness for their wrongdoings, and some have even apologized to the victims of their crimes. Many of them have committed to improving themselves spiritually, physically, and mentally. Some have even taken youngsters under their wings and said, "Hey, don't mess up your life like I did. If you get a chance to walk out this door, stay out and don't come back!"

There is a new day breaking for all of us, and if these incarcerated men and women can find light and hope within the confines of prison walls, how dare those of us who can walk around here freely every day not see the light that shines upon us.

So many of us are incarcerated in the prisons of our own minds by not looking for our own light. We can easily get caught behind the bars of a dead-end job, a lifeless marriage, or a hopeless financial situation. We have to get up every single day and make the choice to focus on the positive. If we choose to focus on the negative, we're not walking toward our light. If we look at our background, our social status, and every mishap that ever happened to us as tragic, we're missing out on the light within that situation.

Look, here's a real light: If you are still waking up every day, it's because God has a greater plan for you and it's not yet completed. Every day is an opportunity to see your light as a gift. We all have opportunities that are presented to us on a daily basis. These opportunities show up in the people we meet, the invitations we receive, or the information shared with us. Our response to these choices can determine the quality of our lives.

## THE OPPORTUNITIES LIE IN YOUR DECISIONS

Let's say we have a young man who decides he's going to join a gang. We can judge him and say that he doesn't have any opportunities. But in reality, he's had opportunities all along. If he had taken the time to finish school, had not quit his job, had not tried out drugs, or had gone to church like his grandmother told him to, he could have had access to a whole other set of opportunities. But let's get real about this thing: If you do what you've always done, your life will not get better. You can't fill out a job application when you're gangbanging or selling drugs. And you can't get access to the right opportunities if you get caught and spend the rest of your life behind bars. The key to our opportunities lies in our decisions. In order to get the opportunities you want, you have to make the decision to change. Unfortunately, change is where a lot of people get uncomfortable.

All of our actions are intertwined, and they prepare us for the moments to come. We don't know when, where, or how our next big moment is going to show up. I believe this is why God doesn't show us the full picture of our lives. If he did, we'd surely mess it up and quit. If God had shown me that I would be homeless and married twice, I would have said, "Not me. What else you got?" If God had given me a sneak preview and allowed me to see that I would lose every single comedy competition that I entered before I eventually made it, I would have said, "You got to be kidding me."

When I was hosting *Showtime at the Apollo*, I remember

introducing Sean "Puffy" Combs for the first time. He comes walking out onstage with these two fat dudes, who I later learned were Biggie Smalls and Lil' Cease, and I said, "What in the world are these guys going to do? These dudes aren't even singing!" I thought they weren't going to make it, but Sean came back the next time, after he had signed his deal for Bad Boy Records, and then he had a whole army of people with him decked out in Bad Boy baseball jerseys.

I look at all the times I've seen people fail and then make it anyway. I look at my own record of how many times I failed. But failure is such a HUGE part of succeeding. If only we understood the necessity of failure. You can't win until you lose. When you look at a great like Michael Jordan, you have to realize that he didn't win six championships by only winning—he had to taste defeat many, many times.

I no longer look at failure as failure. I now see it as valuable, learned, gained experience. It gives me a chance to see that learning *what not to do* is just as valuable as knowing *what to do*. It's a process, but when you can recognize and embrace the process of failure, you get another step closer to yes.

# CHAPTER 3

# Take the Lid Off the Jar

In moving toward your dream, it's necessary to take the lid off the jar. Far too many of us let our age, race, sex, or economic background hold us down and restrict us from dreaming big. But you can't allow yourself to be held down by what your parents did or the limitations in your immediate environment. You have to take the lid off of your expectations and dream big.

Have you ever looked at what happens to a flea when you put it in a jar? The flea jumps only high enough so that its head no longer hits the lid. If those fleas in the jar have baby fleas, the baby fleas are born with the same vertical ability to jump two hundred times their size. However, because they are in an environment where they only see other fleas jumping so as not to hit their heads, they begin to duplicate the behavior in their environment. You can't concern yourself or try to duplicate the action of others around you. You were clearly created and destined to climb, jump, and soar two hundred times your size and even greater.

How often do we allow the impressions of others to affect our direction, our altitude, or our ability? Far too many times we have stunted our own growth, and we have impeded our leap because of the opinions of others. How often do we stop our own progress because we looked to the left or to the right, and based our actions on someone else's ability? Don't get caught in that trap of comparing yourself to someone else. Release yourself from excuses and limitations.

Just like a flea, we are all born with the ability to take huge, vertical leaps. Yet slowly but surely, we let the neighborhood we grew up in or our family's social or economic background affect how high we jump. We become just like those fleas in a jar, and we let our surroundings stop us from reaching our maximum potential. Some of us have been so conditioned to being in the jar of our limitations that, when the lid is finally taken off, we don't know how to dream big. We can't imagine that we deserve anything better than what we already have. But you know what? We were created to live beyond our current jar, regardless of our age, sex, race, or ability. We were designed to jump so high and so hard that we can literally break the lid off wherever we are.

I remember the first time I had a lid put on my limitations. I was in sixth grade, and my teacher asked everyone in the class to write on a piece of paper what they wanted to be when they grew up. Everybody started writing, and I got excited. I knew exactly what I wanted to be when I got older—I wanted to be on TV. I wrote that down on my paper and turned it in. The teacher started calling our names and reading aloud what we wrote. I couldn't wait for her to call me.

When the teacher finally got to my name, she said, "Little Stevie, stand up and come to the front of the room." As I started walking to the front of the class, I just knew I had written something so deep and powerful that she wanted me to share it with everybody. I was a poor kid with hand-me-down clothes and a stuttering problem. This was my chance to show them all what Little Stevie was made of.

When I finally got to the front, she asked me, "Little Stevie, what did you write on your paper?" I stuck out my little chest and responded with the pride of an Olympic Gold Medal winner, "I want to be on TV." But then she confused me when she followed up with "Why did you write that on your paper?" I'm thinking, Well, isn't that what you asked me do? but I respectfully said, "I thought that's what you wanted us to do, so I wrote down that I want to be on TV." My confusion turned into horror when she asked, "Do you know anybody on TV?"

"No, ma'am," I replied.

"Has anybody in your family been on TV?"

I said again, "No, ma'am."

She delivered her final blow when she said, "Stevie, you can't be on TV. You take this paper home and write something more realistic and then bring it back tomorrow."

I was angry. I didn't understand what was going on. She asked me what I wanted to be, not what my parents did or what I saw other people do. I told her what I wanted, and she killed my dream right in front of the class. The teacher called my house before I got home, and as soon as I walked in the door, my mother asked me, "What did you do up at that school today?" I told her what happened and she said, "Boy, why didn't you just write something that that teacher wanted on the paper?" I stood in that kitchen and couldn't understand why my mother was so upset.

In sixth grade, I was still a little flea, dreaming and jumping at two hundred times my size. I wanted to be on TV because of Bill Cosby. When *I Spy* came on, the whole block would clear out just to run home and watch him. After I saw Bill Cosby, I knew I didn't want to be an electrician, a doctor, or a lawyer. I wanted to be funny on TV, just like him. That's all I knew.

When my father came home, my mother told him what happened, and he said, "Well, what's wrong with that? If that boy wants to be on TV, why can't he write that on his paper?" My mom said, "She wants him to write something more believable." To which he replied, "If that's what he wants to be, then she better start believing it." My father told me to go to my room and wait for him there.

When he finally came in, we talked about what the teacher wanted. He told me to get a new piece of paper. We agreed to write the word "policeman" on the new sheet and give it to her the next day. And then he told me to do something that changed my life forever. He said, "Steve, take out that first paper you wrote, put it in your top drawer, and every morning before you go to school and every night before you go to sleep, you read that paper and you believe that one day you will be on TV."

Now when you turn on your TV, seven days a week, Little Stevie is on TV. I didn't allow one lady in the sixth grade with her limited expectations to affect me. I admit it was damaging to me for some time, but I learned how to keep the dream alive.

In one day, someone tried to put the lid on my dreams, and hours later my father blew the lid off for good. At the time, I didn't realize just what my daddy did for me. Parents can be some of the biggest lid droppers by placing limitations on their children. But you have to take the lid off—no matter who put it on or how long it has been there.

## IS YOUR LID STILL ON?

Here are some ways you can tell if the lid is still on in your life:

- If you're not excited about waking up in the morning

- If you're sitting around every day bored out of your mind

- If you have time to do everything that anyone asks you to do

- If you have time to watch all of your scheduled TV programs every week and not miss an episode

· If you're getting plenty of sleep

· If your dreams make sense to everyone around you

· If you can achieve your dreams by yourself

If you recognized any of these behaviors in yourself, or said yes as you read the list, you have to take the lid off your life and start living your dream.

# PART TWO

# Discovering
and
Embracing
Your Gift

# CHAPTER 4

# The Dash Between Perishing and Sacrificing for Your Dream

Proverbs 29:18 reads, "Where there is no vision, the people perish."

Perishing is the dangerous state of living in a mundane existence without even realizing it. There you are, living your comfortable life, going to the same job—day in and day out—doing the same things. You know your routine so well that you can probably do it without thinking. There are no dreams or aspirations in front of you, and if you were fired tomorrow, you wouldn't know how to pursue a better life.

It would be a sad state of affairs to wake up one morning and realize that you have spent years wandering aimlessly in circles, unclear about your purpose, wasting your gift, and destroying your promise. What kind of life is that? You can't afford to go another day without a clear direction and focus for your life. I'm not coming at this from a high-and-mighty place. I'm sharing this with you because I've been in that state of perishing, and I had no idea of how to get out until I created a new vision for my life and committed myself to living that new promise.

When I think back to my earlier days, it's painful to remember how much of my life was disconnected from a real vision. I would take any job just to pay the rent and put gas in my car. I would date anyone who helped me pass the time. When I wasn't working, I was hanging out with people who didn't push me any closer to where I needed to be. I was dying slowly, and had I not created a new vision for my life, I would probably still be in Cleveland working job to job and making people laugh on the weekends.

Perishing is not always about some overdramatic emotional outpour or losing all of your possessions at once. Most often, perishing is a slow, painful process, and if you aren't paying attention, it will trick you into thinking that this is the way things are supposed to be. By failing to have a vision, you are stripping yourself of every possible blessing, relationship, and opportunity. When you sit by and just let your life perish without a vision, it is the most painful kind of death.

## ARE YOU IN A STATE OF PERISH?

How do you know if you are perishing or not? Let's get honest about it. You can't expect to create a new life and a new vision for yourself if laziness is part of your routine. Procrastination will not get the job done. Doing things halfway, improperly, or not at all won't get the job done. Lack of enthusiasm will not get the job done. Unreliability will not get the job done. Being untrustworthy will not get the job done. Any negative trait that derails you from your dreams will not get the job done. Negativity can never be the fuel that drives your gift.

You can also tell if you are perishing if you are the smartest person in your group. If you are the smartest person in the group, you need to get a new group. You cannot be a person who knows it all and can't be told anything, because it will stifle your creativity as well as the creativity of the people around you.

## WHAT ARE YOU GOING TO DO WITH YOUR DASH?

Another way to put your state of perishing into perspective is to realize that one day your life will come to an end. Whether you want to believe it or not, there will be a casket and a hole in the ground with your name on it. The next home-going service at your church could be yours. And the most important thing on that day won't be the amount of flowers that surround your casket or how well the choir sings your favorite hymn. The only thing that will matter is how well you use that dash between the day you were born and the day you die.

I don't want you to spend your days preoccupied with thoughts of death, but I do want you to live your life thinking about how your dash will make a difference in this world. If you've still got breath in your lungs and blood running through your veins, you've got another day to make your dash count. If you're still blessed to wake up and see another day, God has a purpose, a plan, and a destiny for your dash.

The best way to start moving from perishing into your promise is to make what I call Dash Deposits. These are simply efforts you make on a daily basis to reach your destiny and add to your legacy. Reading a book that helps you master your gift is a Dash Deposit. The work you put in to completing a project that was due today is a Dash Deposit. Talking with your family members during dinner instead of watching TV is a Dash Deposit. Any small or large activity or action that adds to the quality of your life and your family's is a Dash Deposit.

How you use your dash is completely up to you. Let today be the day that you make your dash meaningful as it moves you closer to your destiny.

## Success Actions

List three Dash Deposits you plan to do in the next twenty-four hours. Tweet or Instagram me your #DashDeposits to @ActLikeASuccess.

1. _____

_____

2. _____

_____

3. _____

_____

Now that you have some Dash Deposits in your success account, here are a few more yes-and-no questions for you to seriously consider as you move from perishing to reaching your destiny.

1. Regardless of your track record, are you willing to acknowledge, perfect, and use your gift to be successful?

2. Are you open to changing and evolving your thinking around success?

3. Are you willing to change your actions around success?

4. Are you willing to believe that you deserve all the riches that life has to offer?

If you answered no any of the above questions, gift this book to a person who is willing to acknowledge his or her gift. Give it to a friend who you know has been seeking success but has received no satisfaction through his dead-end job. In fact, leave it on the doorstep of a family member who wants to have a healthier marriage or a better relationship with his or her children.

Now, if you answered yes to all of the questions, keep on reading, because we have more work to do!

## MOVING INTO THE LAND OF PROMISE

There's no way you can move from a state of perishing into the Land of Promise if you don't step up and let the world see your gift. What good is it to be a great chef if you're afraid to let someone sample your dishes? What sense does it make to be a great speaker if you won't let the world hear your voice?

It's entirely possible that you could cash in your life savings to pursue your dream and a year later be flat broke. It's not desirable, but your leap of faith could land you back in your parents' basement. But, which is worse—leaping and falling and getting back up, or living your life regretting that you never leaped at all?

You can't let your fear of the unknown keep you from your destiny. If God had told me that my path toward being a successful comedian would include living out of my car, divorce, and facing a $20 million tax bill, trust me, I would have stayed right on the assembly line at the Ford Motor Company. But taking that leap into a foreign territory prepared me to jump higher and further than I could ever have imagined.

## LIVING ON A WING AND A PRAYER

There's going to come a day when your pursuit of living your dream is going to cost more than the money in your checking account and the credit available on your credit card. What's going to stop you from running back to your old boss and asking for your job back? As you pursue your dream, you have to be prepared for the times of lean, as well as the times of plenty. Nobody said that living in the Land of Promise would be easy. When someone gives you a harsh critique or comes to tear down your character, you have to be confident enough to know that what God has for you cannot be taken away because of one person's opinion. Even if your financial responsibilities require you to take on a part-time job to get you over the hump, you have to stay committed to your dream until you get the break you deserve.

## WHEN YOU KNOW THAT YOU KNOW

Nobody but you and God can see it, but you know your gift is in there. It doesn't make sense to most people right now why you're spending so much time on something that looks like a useless hobby, but you know in your heart that it's the key to your future. At the end of the day, your personal resolve to nurture and grow your gift will be the deciding factor between your success and your failure. I don't care how close you are with your mother or how much your best friend supports your dream; if you don't know and believe in your gift for *yourself*, you will never have the life that God has destined for you.

When you are really living in your gift, you just know it. When you are doing what you are meant to be doing, you can just feel it. When the right opportunity comes along, you won't have to force it. I want you to be able to *live* in a space where your dream is no longer a question of who you are but the answer for everything you are meant to be.

## GETTING MOTIVATED AND STAYING FOCUSED

Moving from perishing into the Land of Promise won't work if you aren't motivated to stay there. We think that motivation comes from somewhere else, but our greatest motivation is inside of us. The only difference between successful and unsuccessful people is that successful people know what their gift is and how to focus on it at all costs.

Once I discovered my gift, pursuing it became my sole focus. After I finished focusing on the insignificant stuff and started focusing on my promise, I began to move in the right direction.

We have to commit to taking the lid off our dream every day. Most of the world just wants you to get a job and make someone else rich. Too many schools and training programs will steer you toward serving a company while forgetting about you and your dreams. Blow that lid off of your life *every day* and say to the world, "I might be in this place right now, paying my dues and mastering my craft, but my dreams are out of this world!"

## Success Actions

What is an out-of-the-jar, no-holds-barred dream that you have for your life today? Don't limit your dreams to just your career. Think about your family, your relationships, and your contributions to your community or your house of faith. You've got your ideas? Now write them down here. Make your descriptions come to life with rich detail.

_____

_____

_____

_____

_____

_____

_____

_____

_____

_____

_____

_____

_____

_____

_____

_____

CHAPTER 5

# Not What You Are Paid For, but What You Were Made For

I remember vividly the day that I decided to change my life. It was Tuesday, October 8, 1985, in Cuyahoga Falls, Ohio. I was twenty-seven, married, and a new father of beautiful twin baby girls. While I was excited to be a father for the first time, we were really struggling. We were living in a little two-bedroom house, and I was barely scraping by with my full-time job and writing jokes on the side for comedian A. J. Jamal. One night, I was hanging out in Hilarities Comedy Club with a woman named Gladys Jacobs. She knew about my gig with A.J.

"Why don't you just write some jokes for yourself and sign up for the open-mike night for next week?" she asked. I agreed to sign up for the next show.

I hung around to see Gladys perform her set. There were nine comedians onstage that night with Gladys. Some of the performers were good; some were bad; and, surprisingly, the guy who did Bullwinkle and Popeye impersonations slayed the crowd the most. The host got to the end of the open-mike list, and the last comic was a no-show.

"Well, why don't we just start with the names for next week? If Steve Harvey is here, come on up," he said.

I was sitting there minding my business, eating, and drinking a glass of grapefruit juice. I put down my drink and said, "Gladys, somebody here has the same name."

She looked at me and said, "Fool, he means *you*. Get on up there!"

I ran up onstage and started my set by facing the wall. When I turned around, I said, "I ain't even supposed to be here until next week." To my shock, they started laughing. "No, really, I'm not kidding. This is an accident." The crowd kept on laughing, but Gladys could see that I was freezing up.

"Tell us the story about your boxing days!" she yelled.

I starting telling a story about boxing one of my fiercest opponents, who was named Bernard Taylor. I really got into it and began demonstrating how he used to climb into the ring with a pigeon-toed walk. The crowd was howling. Meanwhile, the host was on the side of the stage motioning for me to wrap it up, but I thought he was telling me to keep going, so I told another story. Finally, I said, "Well, I can't think of anything else to say, so I'll see y'all next week!"

After I finished, the host brought all the contestants back onstage. There was a clap-off for the best comedian. I won my first amateur night. The first-place prize was fifty dollars!

I walked into work the next morning with that fifty dollars, and you couldn't tell me nothing. I marched myself into the card shop downstairs and paid them twenty-five dollars to print up two hundred cards with my name, address, phone number, and the word "Comedian" right under my name. I waited until all two hundred cards were off press. When they were done, I took my fresh box of printed cards and went upstairs to show them to my buddy, Russell.

When I saw Russell, he said, "Where were you last night? I was looking for you and couldn't find you anywhere." I told him that I won an amateur night at a comedy club.

"A comedy club? That's exactly where you need to be!"

I showed him the cards. "I'm thinking of quitting this job."

"Well, don't think about it. Do it!"

I got a box, cleared off my desk, and headed to my boss's office to deliver the news.

"Tom, look, I really appreciate the opportunity, but I have a young family, and last night I discovered what I really want to be."

"Well, what's that, Steve?" my boss asked.

I told him about winning the amateur night at the comedy club and I informed him that I was a comedian now. Tom looked me right in the eye and said, "You won one amateur night and now you think you're a comedian, huh? Steve, I've never heard you say a funny thing since you've been here."

I wanted to show him that I was really serious. I handed him one of my new business cards, which was still warm from the printer.

"Listen, Steve, you're a young guy with a young family to support. Don't go chasing some foolish dream. Now take that box, put your stuff back on your desk, and go sit down. I will pretend like this never happened."

I let Tom talk me right out of quitting. I turned around and left his office. I went back to my desk.

"What are you doing?" asked Russell.

I told him that Tom made some good points about being responsible and taking care of my family.

Russell shot back, "So you're really going to let this dude tell you what to do with your life? Steve, let me ask you something: Is Tom the kind of man you want to be?"

"No."

"Is his car the kind of car you want?"

"No."

"So why in the world are you listening to him? Steve, you're the funniest man I know. I really think you have missed your calling being here. Keep your stuff in that box and go."

I grabbed my box for the second time and headed back to Tom's office. I explained to him again that I was really serious about becoming a comedian. He looked at me like I was the biggest fool in the world.

"All right, Steve. If you walk out that door now, I'm not going to give you your job back." I thanked him again, and I went to shake his hand, but he refused it. "You're making a bad move, Steve, but good luck to you." I walked out that door, jumped, and never looked back.

Now, please don't walk into work tomorrow and quit your job. Let me tell you that during my first few months as a comedian, I thought Tom was right. I made $125 my first month and the second month was even worse, because

I was only seventy-five dollars' worth of funny. I ended up losing my family and my home. I thought it would be better out on the road, but it just got worse, and I barely had enough money to send some back home.

Even in the midst of being homeless, I knew I was doing what I was born to do. I wasn't successful at it yet, but I was on my way. I've known that I had a gift to make people laugh since I was ten, but I didn't attach it to a vehicle called "being a comedian" until I was in my late twenties.

I want to inform you of one very important piece of information: You have a gift! Yes, you have a gift, too. Our creator, in his infinite wisdom, created every single soul with a gift. Your gift is completely unique. No one can rob you of it. You are the only one who can choose to use it or to ignore it. You have the power to permit it to be used to enrich your life.

"Steve, what is *my* gift?" Your gift is the single thing that you do at your absolute best with the least amount of effort.

Take a moment to really think about what I am saying. Be honest with yourself while considering my words: *You have a gift.* Note that I did not ask you what you were passionate about or what you hoped, dreamed, or wished for. What do you do the absolute best with the least amount of effort?

Don't think that a gift is limited to playing sports or performing onstage. There are many other options. Are you a problem solver? Are you a sharp listener who can convey the views of others? Do you have the ability to bring together people who can then form mutually beneficial, business-enhancing relationships? Do you cook well? Are you an excellent mediator? Do you have a calming voice that can lift a person's spirit? Are you especially effective communicating with children? Can you draw or paint? Do you like designing garments? Does creating floral arrangements give you a thrill? What is it that your creator has naturally endowed *you* to do?

This whole notion of "gift" can be challenging. We have been conditioned to care more about jobs and titles. Our gift is not the job we have that we think is better than everyone else's. I have plenty of friends who are making millions of dollars and hate what they do because they are using their talents, but not their gift. As you are figuring out what your gift is, do not be misled by alternate career options.

Some of you may be having trouble identifying your gift because you are attaching it to or defining it as a job. I completely understand that, and I know this is especially true for men because so much of our identity is tied to the company we work for and the title on our business cards.

But your job is not your gift. It may be one of the places where you can use your gift. But you should also be able to use your gift in your relationships, your communities, and throughout every aspect of your life.

Your gift is something that is connected to you whether you are working or vacationing, whether you are with the family or even all alone. Your gift cannot be taken because of downsizing or given to you because someone creates a job description. Your gift exists because you do.

I have come to learn that no single job would ever contain my gift. My gift and your gift are bigger than a single job. I was so preoccupied with getting gigs that I didn't realize that my gift to make people laugh was not about a comedy stage. I have been able to move beyond the "job" I thought was my gift and truly see my unique gift make room for me on radio, TV, movies, and, yes, even in books. Notice that when I'm on the radio, I'm making people laugh. When I'm doing my television show, I'm making people laugh. When I'm hosting *Family Feud*, I'm making people laugh. My gift is always with me, and I use it to increase my success.

If you are a driver, I don't want you to get hung up on "I drive well, so I'll drive for a company." No, your gift is driving, but the right vehicle for your gift may not be driving for a company; it depends on what will give you the most satisfaction. You could be one of the greatest drivers in any area and in any field if driving truly is your gift. You will have the ability to become incredibly successful with your gift driving. I guarantee you that it will be more exciting for you to wake up in the morning and drive for yourself or spend your day developing younger drivers who will work for you. Or maybe the right vehicle for your gift will be providing transportation for your local church or the elderly members of your community. See, your gift doesn't have to become a profession. It could be something that you do on a volunteer basis to serve your community. If serving brings you pleasure, you are already rewarded by the joy it brings into your life.

Your gift may be to serve. Your whole life, people have told you that the only place your gift makes sense is at church or in the nonprofit sector. Well, that may be the place for you to thrive or the place to which you feel called.

There is a huge service industry. I can't tell you how many service people, from the door to the executive office, make my life better in hotels, restaurants, spas, and event venues. You could one day own your own hotel or be the general manager of the best restaurant in your city. All it takes is the gift of service you have to allow you to make people's lives more enjoyable.

## WHAT YOUR GIFT IS NOT

Passion is a strong emotion associated with something you do. Passion is the emotion, but it is never the gift. Some people are not passionate about their gift because they have not yet given themselves the room to actually walk in it yet. I want you to have passion for your gift as you learn to acknowledge it and perfect it, but do not confuse the passion you have for something else as your gift.

Finally, your gift is not your talents. In fact, what we do well sometimes blocks us from finding out what we do great. I think of talents as the lesser to one's gift. Talents can be learned while a gift is inherent. Your gift cannot be studied by another and then performed at the same proficiency. However, our talents often lead us to exercising our gift.

Use your talents, but know that it will be your gift that puts you in the presence of great people. Proverbs 18:16 says, "Your gift will make room for you and put you in the presence of great men."

After you identify your gift and decide to use it, your gift will lead to the fulfillment of your life's purpose and mission. Presented before you will be a wonderful opportunity to live a life of riches. Your success will be tied to the gift that you were freely given on the day you were born. Your gift will unlock all of the mysteries of your life. Your mission, your purpose, and your destiny will all be tied to one thing—*your gift*. I guarantee that your whole life will have new meaning and direction when you recognize your gift and decide upon the most valuable way to use it.

Take a minute to answer the following questions to help you identify your gift.

## Success Actions

1. What is the thing that you do at your absolute best with the least amount of effort?

_____

_____

_____

_____

_____

_____

_____

**2.** What is that one gift that other people associate with you? Why?

_____

_____

_____

_____

_____

_____

_____

**3.** If you followed the advice of these other people, how have you utilized your gift?

_____

_____

_____

_____

_____

_____

_____

# CHAPTER 6

# Knowing Your Gift and Putting It into the Right Vehicle

S teve Jobs was truly one of the greatest American innovators of the last thirty years. He was a master at creating technology that you didn't even know you needed until he showed you how it would revolutionize your life. Every time you enter an Apple store and open a box with the Apple logo on it, you know that you will get a little bit of that Steve Jobs' magic in your hands.

Steve Jobs had a gift for seeing technology in ways that actually changed the way we live our lives. Some of you are even addicted to your iPhones and iPads.

The ability to innovate and transform technology was both Steve Jobs's gift and the mark that he left on the world. This combination of using your gift and infusing it with your personal skills and talents is what I call your gift mark.

Similar to a trademark, your gift mark is the stamp that you leave on the world every time you use your God-given talents and skills at your highest capacity. You know without a doubt what to expect every time you purchase a box with an Apple logo or sit behind the wheel of a car with that BMW insignia. Your gift mark should be what people come to expect *every* time they hire you or ask you to be part of their team. Your gift mark is the flavor you add to your gift, showing the world that it has your DNA in it. When you sit down at the table, people know that they will receive your gift in just the way that only you can deliver it.

If you are an event planner, someone should be able to come into one of your get-togethers and immediately see your gift mark expressed in the manner in which your table settings are displayed, or reflected in the warm lighting in the room. If you are a life coach, someone should be able to see a unique transformation in the business and personal lives of your clients that reflects your special energy. Your gift mark is what will separate you from the pack.

You can have two barbers who know how to do a mean shape-up. But the difference between the one who has clients lining up to get into his chair and the one who can't keep a chair is the gift mark. The good barber's gift mark could be as simple as knowing how to connect with one customer or remembering that another customer's son has a sensitive scalp.

Once you uncover your gift, find that distinctive touch that will make your gift stand out and shine. What you do with your gift is completely up to you. I recommend that you harness it to share with the world in a variety of ways.

It is never too late to embrace your gift. I recognize that most people, even you, are just a few steps away from the start of turning what could have been into what can be.

After you have identified your gift, you need to look around you to discover the right vehicle for your gift. The right vehicle will give you the transportation you need to navigate your journey and advance you into your future. As you begin to search for the right outlets for your gift, you will realize that they are everywhere around you. The people who are truly successful use the vehicle that is right for today to work toward the next upgrade that will lead to an even higher rung of success.

## YOUR TODAY VEHICLE

What I loved most about Beyoncé's self-titled surprise digital release was not the music. It wasn't that she shocked the world and just decided to forgo all the typical marketing and promotions and just drop it like . . . *Pow!* I loved that it was full of images of Beyoncé the child singer, and the road she took to become Beyoncé the stadium filler. There is a clip of her in a group called Girls Tyme. In a competition, they lost to a boys' band no one ever heard of again. In this day and age, when stars, business moguls, and even athletes pretend that they became hits overnight, it deceives people into believing they have to connect their gift to a million-dollar vehicle immediately. Most people never heard of Girls Tyme, but that was just *one* of the vehicles Beyoncé used before Destiny's Child, before Sasha Fierce, and before Mrs. Carter. Beyoncé used the vehicle that was available to her at the moment to work toward the next opportunity of her lifetime.

You do not have to bog down your journey by trying to find a vehicle that will get you all the way to your final destination. The first vehicle that you initially attach yourself to may not be the one that finishes your journey. Simply attach yourself to a vehicle that gets your gift into motion. Think about this in terms of traveling on a city bus from one location to the next. Often you have to get a transfer in order to complete the journey. You will then be led to another transfer, which will take you to your second vehicle.

I didn't attach my gift to a vehicle called being a comedian until I was nearly thirty years old. My first endeavor was a free amateur night. My next trip was a paying gig for twenty-five dollars. Now, a twenty-five-dollar vehicle certainly could not get me to the level I am at today. But it was a start. The transfer came when I became a featuring act, which took me from $350 per week to $750 per week.

The next transfer I caught led me to be a national headliner earning anywhere from $1,500 a week in small comedy clubs to upwards of $60,000 in larger venues. My next transfer led me to a lifestyle of earning $25,000 per night.

My next transfer led me to become the host of *Showtime at the Apollo*. From there, that venture gave me national TV exposure, which then led to a TV show called *Me and the Boys*. That show then led me to *The Steve Harvey Show*. After that, I became one of the original Kings of Comedy. That platform propelled me into the stratosphere of what I set out to be in the first place—one of the premier stand-up comedians in the country.

Are you so busy looking for the luxury vehicle now that your new budget gift can't afford it? I need you to be open to connecting to a vehicle that complements the current level of your gift and can move you to the next level. That means begin now, where you are. Where can you start today to begin the journey? What simple steps or vehicle can you attach yourself to?

Let's say you are a hairdresser. Can you start by doing hair in your kitchen? Can you move up to get a booth or a chair at a local salon? Are you willing to do the work to get your cosmetology license? Are you willing to learn under somebody who knows more than you do? Don't ever be afraid to put yourself in a lesser position so that you can learn something from someone who knows more. No one can teach you more than someone who has already been there.

You're not Vidal Sassoon at this point, but you are well on your way. Keep working and catch another transfer. Get a better chair at a better salon. Get another transfer and get into partnership with another girl or guy. Catch another transfer. Start a small storefront salon. Catch another transfer. Get more chairs in your salon. Catch another transfer. Start renting out booth space in your salon. As my father used to say, "Inch by inch everything is a cinch."

If you are a truck driver and your dream is to own a

fleet of trucks, you can't wait until someone gives you the money to purchase your first fleet. Initially, you have to get your commercial driver's license. After you get your chauffeur's license, then you can begin driving on a local level. Then you can begin driving on an interstate level.

Once your start building up your cash, you can save to purchase your first truck. After you get that first truck and become known for being a driver who delivers on time, you have to think about buying another truck and hiring another driver. Your dream is right on track. You just keep purchasing transfers from one vehicle to the next. Before you know it, you've got ten trucks on the road and your dream of owning your own interstate transportation company becomes a reality.

If your dream is to be a chef, start cooking for your family. Talk to people who are looking to do special family events but who can't yet afford an expensive caterer. Volunteer to cook at an assisted-living center in the area, or create a program at the local middle school to teach kids to cook. Who knows, you may get on the local news for what you are doing with the kids. Your appearance could be an opportunity for you to share your vision with the world. Those local vehicles are the perfect places to get started.

I personally know the gentleman who creates the floral

arrangements for the Four Seasons hotels throughout the world. He didn't start his career flying from New York to Paris to Dubai to share his gift for arranging flowers. That gift started by working in a much smaller hotel that didn't really appreciate the talent that he brought to their staff. But he didn't let their lack of appreciation stop him from doing what he was called to do. Before he knew it, someone saw one of his creations and gave him the opportunity to design the arrangements for the Four Seasons, and now he also prepares floral arrangements for the Grammys and *The Queen Latifah Show.*

Just because you sing well doesn't mean that you have to use your gift to become the next Whitney Houston or Mariah Carey. Having the ability to make people laugh doesn't mean you need to be a stand-up comic. If you've seen the Academy Award–winning documentary *20 Feet from Stardom*, you know that the greatest voices of our generation tore up the stage as background singers for some of the biggest performers in the world. And the best comics aren't always the ones in front of the mike; they are often the ones behind the scenes writing the jokes.

Your gift might be to teach, and you've avoided going down the path because most classroom teachers aren't paid what they're worth. But who said you have to teach in a classroom? Motivational speaker Lisa Nichols is also a teacher, and she empowers sold-out crowds all over the country. Tony Robbins is a teacher, and I know most of you wouldn't mind having a piece of his educator paycheck. Finding the right vehicle for your gift will be the key to moving your gift from a dream to a reality. Both Lisa and Tony realized that they have to create their own paths, not let someone else create them, and not fall back on what the generation before them did.

## LET YOUR VEHICLE TEACH YOU HOW TO DRIVE

Your vehicle doesn't just connect to your gift and transport you to the next level of your success. Your vehicle should accentuate your gift. It should help you to perfect your gift. This means that you have to be aggressive about learning how to drive and be patient enough to master the vehicle you are in before you trade up to the next. Master that gift where you are. Make every mistake you can in the lemon before you get the coupe.

## THINK BIGGER THAN THE RIDE YOUR PARENTS DROVE

My dad was a car man. He owned a '50-something Mercury, an old '63 woodie station wagon, and a '68 station wagon, which became my first car when he passed it on to me in 1977. I don't want you to get stuck in one vehicle. You must recognize that it is about getting you to the next level, and not about taking you the whole way. I have seen too many smart, talented, gifted people stay in the same vehicle too long. If you notice that you are working hard and smart, connected to a vehicle and clear on your vision, but every day you seem to move less and less, it's time to upgrade. It's time to take another class, join a new organization, or start a new business. Look, if you are committed to your gift, and you are growing and perfecting it, you will know when your gift is becoming too much for the vehicle.

## DON'T BE AFRAID TO TAKE A TEST DRIVE

Now that you have started using the vehicles available to master your gift, it is time to start choosing the avenue that will get you to higher levels. Let's get beyond thinking of vehicles for our gifts as just traditional nine-to-five jobs. You have to take the time to test-drive as many options as you can for your gift. And don't be afraid to choose a plane when others are driving a car. Your vehicle can be as unique as your gift. When I started out as a comedian back in the '80s, you couldn't have told me that I would have several opportunities for my gift, including hosting a radio show, having my own daytime television show, taking over a popular game show, and now writing my third book.

We also can't be afraid to test-drive a car outside our price range. Some of us won't even think about sitting in a luxury car because we can see only where we are now. We can be too quick to shut down a vehicle because it requires working longer hours, learning a new skill set, or spending more time away from home. Even though a vehicle might require a greater investment up front, you have to consider how smooth your gift will move you through your journey if you are willing to put it in a high-quality vehicle.

## DON'T GET STUCK WITH A LEMON

Just as important as knowing what kind of vehicles will be best suited for your gift is knowing what opportunities to avoid. Just because you are a great chef, it doesn't necessarily mean that you need to open a restaurant. The best vehicle for your gift could be catering private affairs. If you are a great basketball coach, the best outlet for your gift could be coaching high school students instead of setting your sights on the NBA.

I'm the last person to dampen anyone's desire to become an entrepreneur, but I want you to think hard about entrepreneurship before you sign on the dotted line. This isn't just any ordinary ride. Entrepreneurship requires sacrifices beyond the responsibilities of working a nine-to-five job. You're going to need the right team to keep you on track. There are likely expenses that require resources that you do not have to invest at the moment. Or maybe you're the kind of person who prefers quality time for yourself and your family, and less time spent working long hours. And you can't just let anybody into your car when you are committed to being an entrepreneur. Do you know what a person on a plane is called who doesn't want to go where it's going? A hijacker.

There's nothing wrong with paddling the canoe of an entry-level position while keeping your eyes on the yacht of entrepreneurship. Take the time to network with people who are in your field. Find out what it really takes to become your own boss and what kind of sacrifices of time, money, and energy it will take to be successful.

### Success Actions:
### Choosing the Right Vehicle

Ask yourself these questions in order to choose the perfect vehicle for you and your gift.

1. Where is your final destination? It is important that you always keep in mind where you want to end up.

_____

_____

_____

_____

_____

_____

_____

_____

_____

_____

**2.** Where is your next stop? What is your next goal? Is it a promotion at your current job? Is it going out on your own and doing a side project? Is it starting a family? See, this is the key question. Because the opportunity or vehicle for Robert—who is thirty, single, looking to be married, and wants a job that pays well but gives him plenty of family time—will not be the same vehicle for Stephanie—who is the same age, doesn't want a family, and wants to be partner in a huge corporate law firm. What do *you* want? Can this get you to that place and set you up for the next trip?

_____

_____

_____

_____

_____

_____

_____

_____

_____

3. Do you know how to operate this vehicle *today* just enough not to crash? That means you are not growing. Don't go back to being a teacher in your old school when you know your next stop is principal. Is the vehicle out of your mastery, but controllable? That's the drive you want. It's challenging, fun, takes you out of your comfort zone, *but* . . . you can make it work. That's where you need to be.

_____

_____

_____

_____

_____

_____

_____

_____

_____

_____

_____

These questions will make sure you are focused on the right vehicle for you. This will also keep you from trying to buy matching Bugattis with a friend who isn't even going to the same place that you're going. Tailor your vehicle for your gift and your journey, and you will always be in the right ride.

## Success Actions

List the best vehicles for your gift *today*.

_____

_____

_____

_____

_____

_____

_____

_____

_____

Write down the kind of vehicles that you would like to use for your gift five to ten years from now.

Share one of your new rides with me using the hashtag #Vehicle4MyVictory@ActLikeASuccess.

# CHAPTER 7

# Understanding
# the Makeup of You

I n order for you to properly fuel your gift, you have to embody the proper makeup, and often that requires some change on your part. When I refer to makeup, I'm not talking about the thousands of dollars you ladies spend on Revlon or MAC, or how much you men spend on Brooks Brothers; I'm talking about your getting the right caliber of traits together that will lead you to your biggest dreams. Your makeup is the driving force behind the vehicle you have attached yourself to that will lead you to success. In this chapter, we are going to explore what it takes to develop your personal makeup to the highest levels and propel you forward to reach your goals.

## WHAT KIND OF MAKEUP DO YOU NEED?

The first thing you need in your makeup kit is to be the kind of person who attracts rather than repels others. There are no self-made men; therefore, you have to learn the laws of attraction to draw the right people to you. You have to be easy to work with, or at least be willing to create the atmosphere that makes it easy to work with you.

Next, you have to aspire to be a visionary person with a positive outlook. Those who allow other people to expand, develop, and explore are the kinds of people you want to have around you. When you are with the right people, there are ripe opportunities for you to gain from their experiences and knowledge.

You also must recognize your shortcomings and be willing to improve on them. In recognizing your shortcomings, you may want to consider them when hiring others to be a part of your team.

Finally, you have to respect time—yours and others'—by being punctual. You have to be a person of integrity. You have to be honorable and reliable by doing what you say you're going to do when you say you're going to do it.

## GET HONEST, GET REAL, AND GET NEW HABITS

An essential part of your makeup has to be getting honest, getting real, and being willing to take on new actions.

### Get Honest

Now is not the time to start lying to yourself. If you are tired of the way you've been living, it's time to give that up. I want you to go to a mirror right now, look yourself in the eye, and be honest with where you are right now. Don't reason it away. Don't blame it on somebody else. What is the thing you do that keeps blocking you? Look beyond your excuses and ask yourself, Why? Your answers may be fear, failure, family circumstances, or finances. If the answers don't immediately come to you, this may be the time to seek pastoral or professional counseling. Don't be afraid to get the help you need in order to live the life you deserve.

## Get Real

This is where we get to the good part of replacing your negative actions with positive ones. Is procrastination killing you? Replace it with a strategy that will get you into action. Do you refuse to admit when you are wrong? Enlist a partner or a friend to keep you accountable for your responsibilities. Whatever the issue, make a commitment to get real and find positive and responsible replacement actions.

Here's the problem with people who think that they have a makeup that they really don't have. If you're asking the question and answering it, too, you don't have the real makeup. You can't have the real answer. All you are doing is constantly telling yourself what you want to hear about you. You have to be willing to have a bone-chillingly honest conversation with yourself. By not being frank about the situation, the only person you are cheating is you.

## Get New Habits

Once you have become honest with yourself and you identify new actions for tackling your weaknesses, here comes the hard part—changing your habits. In his book *Making Habits, Breaking Habits*, psychologist Jeremy Dean challenges the myth that it takes only twenty-one days to change a habit. It might take two years to fully make a shift in some areas of your life, but that's now two productive years for a lifetime of reward.

Don't worry about how much time it takes to make the shift. Time is in your favor when you use it productively. Focus your energy on developing your new habits. Just take it one day at a time. And when you get done with one day, I want you to do something revolutionary—I want you to get up and do it again. And again. And again. Pretty soon, this won't just be some new habit you're trying to conquer—this will be your new road map for success.

## CHANGING YOUR MAKEUP WITH INTEGRITY

Many times in my life I have had to change my makeup. I had to start becoming a more positive person with integrity to get the job done. I think the biggest shift for me was during a joke-writing period. I learned a lot from Richard Pryor. What made Richard Pryor so great was his openness. He was willing to talk about all of it—his growing up around after-hours joints, his catching on fire, the arguments in the car, and his marital issues. That's what made him most effective.

When I began in comedy, I was so protective of who I was and where I came from. I was trying to write my jokes in the fashion that others wrote, and as a result I didn't develop the truth of who I was as a stand-up comedian. Once I was no longer afraid to open up about me and my truth, things changed for me professionally. Talking about my truth allowed me to expand my material. I was no longer afraid to talk about my mother, who taught Sunday school; or my failed marriages; or my growing up in Cleveland. This was the first time I came face-to-face with real integrity.

As we grow our integrity, one of the first pieces to focus on is learning how to lead. We get too focused on looking to other people at times when the real answers lie inside of us. We have to take the time to recognize our own strengths and weaknesses. I think what makes me effective as a person of integrity on the radio or as a spokesperson is that people know I am going to tell them the truth no matter what that truth is. You don't always have to agree with it, but I'm telling you my truth. I think that people have grown to respect that.

## GIVING YOURSELF A REAL SELF-EVALUATION

Improving your makeup also means that you have to be willing to give yourself a real self-evaluation. When I write a joke and I go out onstage, I give a joke three shots before I decide to throw it away or keep it. If I tell the joke and it always gets a big laugh, I rate that joke a 1. If I tell it and it gets a laugh only sometimes, then that joke is a 2. If I tell a joke and most of the time it doesn't get a laugh, that's a 3. When I first started, I needed those jokes because I needed the time. You're paid fifteen minutes to open, thirty minutes for the middle set, and forty-five minutes to headline. I needed this time so I could become a headliner. I learned that if you are out there telling 3's, that's a shaky set. So every time I wrote a new joke and it was a 2, I got rid of a 3. The only way I did that was to have an honest assessment with myself. I kept writing jokes, and when I got a 1, I would get rid of a 2. After a few years, I had all 1's. That's when I really started developing as a stand-up: when I created that system of self-evaluation.

Your personal self-evaluation has to be one of complete and total honesty. The only one who can do the self-evaluation is you. Until you are ready to have a completely honest conversation, even a self-evaluation will do you no good.

I know that I'm not great with mundane tasks. I have to hire somebody around me who is good at the day-to-day details. I also know that I'm not good with graphs and charts. I learned that in college. You cut the lights and put a graph on the wall, then I'm going to go to sleep. So I hire people who like graphs. I don't like having to repeat myself over and over again to get a person to understand something. I don't have the patience for it. I also have to constantly watch myself and work on not coming up short. Real integrity is knowing where your shortcomings are.

## SETTING THE RIGHT BALANCE

Your core makeup also has to have the right balance. Through all of my experiences I have learned that the following order is essential for every successful person:

- God

- Family

- Education

- Business

If you prioritize your life in that order, success is yours on whatever level you want. In my life I have come to realize that God has to be first. I used to have business first, education second, family third, and God last. Until I got that order right, I couldn't get my life together.

After putting God first, you have an obligation to take care of your family. You cannot have children and not take care of them. How do you expect the universe to take care of you if you don't start by taking care of your child? How do you think more blessings will come to you if you won't take care of the blessings you've already been given? Regardless of the relationship you have with your child's mother or father, you are obligated to take care of that life. Same thing applies to your husband or your wife.

Once you have God and family in the right order, now you need to focus on education. When I refer to education, that doesn't always mean going to a four-year institution. You should always be educating yourself about your gift and whatever business you are in. You may have to go back to school to get a certificate of training in your area of interest. For me, there was no school for learning how to do comedy. My education was watching the greats of comedy to see what they did to become great. I had to spend a lot of time observing what other comedians before me did.

I also had to spend a lot of time educating myself about

show business. The term "show business" really needs to be recognized as two separate words. If I have a great show, it is because everybody who came to see me enjoyed themselves. But there's no business in show business if I don't know how to book myself and charge for my shows appropriately. It could be a great show, but without the proper steps in place, there is no business. On the flip side, I could have a good business sense and know how to get booked everywhere, but if I'm not funny, I won't be invited back.

## BE OPEN TO WHAT COMES NEXT

Another part of your makeup that is essential for your success is learning how to be open. You can't get so stuck in how you do things that you aren't open to seeing and doing things in a different way.

Some of you may feel like you already have your life together. Let me be the first to tell you congratulations. Now that you have it all together, let me ask you this: What's next? Knowing what's next is paramount to your success. The what's next is the reason to keep waking up. The what's next is the driving force for all successful people. There always has to be a what's next.

You might already be a millionaire. Again, congratulations on your success. But in order to stay a millionaire you have to make more millions. You can't sell the same book. You can't tell the same joke. You can't keep singing the same song. You have to write a new book, tell a new joke, sing a new song.

So, I ask you again—what's next? There has to be a reason to get up tomorrow. There has to be a reason to go forward. Your calling has to be stronger than your current circumstances to help your dream keep moving forward.

## WHAT OTHER MAKEUP DO YOU NEED?

Every person's unique gift will dictate how he or she will operate in the world. Someone who specializes in working with children will need to be patient and caring, while stockbrokers will need to be sharp, exact, and quick on their feet. If you aren't sure what traits you need to work on, think about the skills for which people give you the most compliments. Are you good with details, great at connecting with new people, or proficient at setting up a good meeting? Catalog your skills and put in the work to make them even better.

Next, take stock of the characteristics that people constantly tell you that you need to improve on. For example, are you prone to skipping steps, or do you become frustrated during tight deadlines? Don't just chalk up poor characteristics to "Well, that's just the way I am." Remember that perfecting your character is as much a part of your development as executing your gift.

Outside of taking your own self-inventory, who are the people you admire and respect in your industry, your house of worship, or your community? Talk to them about how they learned to stay cool under pressure, or ask them about the makeup they used to become the type of leaders they are. Trust me, they didn't get to where they are overnight, and any good leaders worth their salt will be more than willing to pour good wisdom and knowledge into your life to help you grow and succeed.

Be the kind of man or woman you want to be by taking on the right makeup, which will make room for your gift and lead you to the best opportunities for expanding it to an even wider audience and a bigger stage.

# CHAPTER 8

# Climbing the Mountain to Reach Your Dreams

There is a Scripture in Psalms that says, "The steps of a good man [or woman] are ordered by the Lord." I interpreted this Scripture in my life to mean that walking into my destiny is a step-by-step process. I truly believe that God provides all of us with the right steps to get to the right place at the right time. As we continue uncovering how to maximize your gift and finding the best opportunities for using your talents, we're now going to look at how to turn these steps into practical goals for your future.

We all have dreams about the life that we truly want to live. Some people take the leap of faith to walk into their dreams, while others remain on the sidelines waiting for a magical moment to happen. What separates the dreamers from the doers? *Goals.* I don't care how vivid your dreams are: Without goals, your dreams will remain a someday phenomenon instead of today's reality. Goals are the key ingredient that helps us stay focused, consistent, and diligent on our path to achieving our dreams.

## CLIMBING THE MOUNTAIN OF SUCCESS

Another way to think about moving your dreams into goals is to imagine that you are climbing a mountain. Your dream is the summit. Every good mountain climber starts out on his journey with his mind focused on the summit. Every step forward, every pull of the rope, and even every pause to regain energy is executed by focusing on his goal. Once he reaches the top, he takes a moment to rest, regroup, refuel, and relish in his victory. But every true climber knows that this is just another leg of the bigger journey. Reaching one summit can never be it for the true climber—each time that he pushes his lungs harder, climbs higher, and scales an even more dangerous rock, he knows that it's just preparation for the next journey.

Wherever you are on the mountain—the top, the bottom, midway up, at the rest stop, at the first-aid station, or even poised to stick the flag in the summit—trust and believe that I have been at all those places in my life. I have stuck the flag in the summit. I have been at the rescue station, the first-aid station. I have been halfway up and fallen all the way back down. I have been caught in a cave. I have fallen in between the cracks and crevices of the mountain. I have been trapped on the mountain. I have been covered by an avalanche on the mountain. You name it, on this mountain, I have done it all. I have been told to not even bother climbing because, they said, I didn't have what it takes to make the climb.

I want you to start thinking of your goals as your personal climb to the top of your dream mountain. You can't just expect to wake up tomorrow and become a millionaire, or have your product be a worldwide sensation overnight, or get the position you have been coveting. What goals are you willing to put in place to make your dreams come true?

I know that goals can often be overwhelming if you take in the full picture at one time, but think about how you can break down your climb into smaller sections. You know yourself better than anyone else, so be honest about what will keep you motivated and inspired. Do you need to take this journey with someone else to ensure that you will keep your word? Will it be better to go solo to stay focused? What kind of milestones do you need to keep yourself on track? Are there better times to execute certain parts of your journey than others? These are good questions to keep in mind as you work your way toward your dream.

Goals are essential because they give you realistic, measurable, and specific targets. They are necessary benchmarks that give you the energy, confidence, and assurance to keep moving in the right direction toward your dream. They can also serve as a handy map for attaining your dreams.

## LET'S GET GOALING

If step one in your journey to become a small-business owner is to do research with a shop owner whom you admire, then pick up the phone, input the number, and have that conversation. A goal is *not* saying, "Yeah, I've been meaning to talk with Mr. Smith about opening my own shop," and then allowing that statement to fall flat by not following up with some action.

You also have to set up your goals in a way that ensures

your success. I know you're excited now that you have this book in your hands and you can really see yourself opening up that bookstore and café you've always dreamed of. But don't sprint out of the gate to apply for that small-business loan or seek angel investors if you don't have a solid business plan in place. I definitely want you to make big goals, but don't make them so far outside your comfort zone that you set yourself up for failure. If you honestly don't know where to begin, start by just setting up a regular time in your calendar to focus on your dream. If you have an hour to yourself after you drop the kids off at soccer practice, sit down in your favorite spot and make that your goal time. If there is someone in your church or your community group whom you can recruit for some conversations, allow them to help you chart out your goal process.

Your goals also need to be tailored to your gift, your skill set, and your lifestyle. I don't expect a forty-year-old, married mom of three to work toward her goals at the same pace as a twenty-five-year-old single man. The woman has an entirely different set of responsibilities that may require more members on her team to help her achieve her goals. By the same token, the twenty-five-year-old man may need more mentors and visionaries to make up for his lack of experience. Create your goals for *you*. Don't waste your energy dwelling on how someone else did what you want to do or how fast they made their goal a reality. Embrace *your* journey and the path God has for *you*.

## HOW SMART ARE YOUR GOALS?

One of the most popular methods for creating good goals is the SMART method. SMART stands for Specific, Measurable, Attainable, Relevant, and Time-Sensitive. Here are some key steps to keep in mind as you put the SMART method in place for your goals:

- **MAKE YOUR GOALS SPECIFIC.** Your goals are not just other random ideas floating around in your head. Your goals must be well defined and crystal clear. Create your goals with your ultimate summit— your dream—in mind.

- **DEFINE YOUR MEASURES.** Now that you've taken your goal out of your head and brought it closer to reality, how will you measure your success? Will it be getting new certifications over the next six months? Or will you increase your customer base for your side gig by 25 percent so that you can make this your full-time income within the next two years? Put your measures into real dates, times, and amounts so that you can quantify your goals. If you're a person who needs some fire under you to keep going, ask a like-minded person to hold you accountable for your measures.

· **AIM FOR THE ATTAINABLE . . . AND THEN STRETCH A LITTLE MORE.** As you start out on your journey toward success, your goals should be attainable *and* should push you outside your comfort zone. For example, if you are in the process of courting investors to take your business to the next level, set up a conversation with that "big person" who you would never think would be interested in your business plan. He or she just may surprise you and get on board with an investment to knock your socks off, and you will surprise yourself by learning just how big you can be in the pursuit of your dream.

· **GET REAL AND RELEVANT.** There is nothing worse than having a goal that has you running in circles. Make your goals relevant to your finish line. If you are committed to launching your idea on social media, don't waste your time posting and liking things on Facebook. Get your priorities straight and stay focused on goals that will keep you moving forward.

- **TAILOR YOUR TIME.** Your goals must have a deadline. When I started out as a comedian, there were certain goals I had each year for the kind of money that I wanted to make in the industry. Not that I was solely focused on the dollar amount, but having time-related benchmarks helped me to create better comedy sets, network with more people in the industry, and carve out a solid path for my future.

## SET UP YOUR GOALS FOR THE NEXT LEVEL

Once you start achieving your goals using the SMART method, what's next? Next, I'm going to introduce you to the SETUP process. The SETUP process is simply asking yourself the following questions as you begin knocking out your goals:

1. What will be my next goal?

2. What will be my target and timetable for the next goal?

3. How will this goal prepare me for the next milestone?

4. If goal A doesn't work, how can I put myself in a better position to achieve goal B or goal C?

5. Whom can I partner with to make the next step happen at a higher quality or a quicker pace?

## CREATING YOUR SUCCESS LADDER

As I mentioned at the start of this chapter, your goals should be a step-by-step process tailored just for you. You can't expect to use my ladder to get to where you are going, and I can't expect to use yours. The key is to have the right number of steps that will be attainable and have just the right amount of challenge to keep you motivated and moving forward.

1. **WRITE DOWN YOUR DREAMS!** If you do not have your dreams written down, they might as well not exist. Whether you are a no-tech, low-tech, or high-tech person, keep your goals with you in a way that works for you and your lifestyle.

2. **CREATE A LIST OF GOALS UNDER EACH DREAM.** Your dream will immediately come alive when you specify the goals that you need to make your dreams come true. One of my goals is for *The Steve Harvey Show* to earn a 3.5 rating. For those of you who are not familiar with the television industry, earning a 3.5 means that I have an average of 3.5 million viewers per show. I have the number "3.5" sown into the cuffs of hundreds of pairs of pants so that every time I step into them, I am stepping out on faith and believing that my show will become a 3.5. When I hit that goal, my earning potential will go to another level. Here is a working set of goals that I am developing for my team and me:

**DREAM:** Earn a 3.5 rating for the 2014–2015 season.

**GOALS:**

- Schedule two working retreats with production staff during summer 2014 to add three new segments to the show.
- Add weekly segment with Lisa Nichols for new "Motivational Monday" segment.
- Create a more robust social media plan to expand the show's reach on Facebook, Twitter, and Instagram.

3. **CREATE A TIMETABLE WITH YOUR DREAM SUMMIT IN MIND.** Imagine where you want to be in the next five years, and begin creating your goals from the perspective of achieving that dream. For example, let's say you want to write your first book in the next three years. Map out the development of that book over a three-year period, so you can track your progress.

4. **GET SMART AND SET UP YOUR GOALS WITH POWER.** Using the SMART method and the SETUP process are powerful ways to make your goals practical and attainable. Walk through the steps that we covered in the previous section to ensure

that you are creating goals that you can achieve and be proud of.

5. **PRIORITIZE YOUR GOALS.** I want you to be excited about your goals. But I don't want you to neglect your family, your health, and your overall well-being in the process. Working toward your dream doesn't mean that you get so laser focused that you lose sight of your priorities. Create your goals in such a way that you can still be a great parent, a great spouse, and, yes, even a dedicated employee while you are planning your exit strategy. And it's okay if prioritization means making smaller steps so that you can have balance in your life. If all you can do is save five hundred dollars toward your dream this year, you're now five hundred dollars closer to putting your gift into the right vehicle.

6. **CELEBRATE YOUR PROGRESS.** For every goal you achieve along the way, celebrate your journey. Often we get so caught up in reaching the summit that we forget to stop as we take in the journey and acknowledge our accomplishments. You have to be your first cheerleader on the road toward success. If you like to journal, create a Goals

Journal to capture your progress. Create this journal as your personal space to articulate your thoughts, feelings, frustrations, and triumphs. If you need to process your journey with another person or other people, set up a regular celebration checkpoint with your team so that they can take pride in your accomplishments, too. Celebrating your goals is as much about honoring your work as it is a source of motivation to keep you moving forward.

The end of your success ladder may be hosting your own inspirational podcast or setting up fitness classes to help seniors in your building get healthy. Whatever your dream is, don't let it swirl around in your head as just another lofty thought. Create goals for your dream that will make your gift come alive. As the saying goes, "Goals are dreams with their feet on the ground." Take this chapter and use these steps to put some feet up under your wildest dreams.

*Success Actions*

What dream are you committed to fulfilling this year?

_____

_____

_____

_____

_____

_____

_____

_____

_____

_____

_____

_____

_____

Create SMART goals for your dream:

**S**pecific: _____

_____

_____

**M**easurable: _____

_____

_____

**A**chievable: _____

_____

_____

**R**ealistic: _____

_____

_____

**T**ime-Sensitive: _____

_____

_____

# CHAPTER 9

# You Have to See It
# to Believe It

Nothing disappoints me more than hearing people filled with big dreams but without goals or vision to make them a reality. Having a vision comes down to one thing: Do you know where you want to go? You have to be clear about your vision because it will drive everything else you do.

Here's a quote that I love from Albert Einstein: "Imagination is everything. It is the preview of life's coming attractions." Your imagination *is* everything. If your focus is on where you are right now, then your right now becomes your forever. Until you change your focus and elevate your imagination, your present situation *will* define you. If imagination is everything, we have to start by changing how we view the coming attractions.

## CREATING A FIRST-CLASS VISION

No matter how much we achieve, we have to keep pushing our imagination. Back in 2001, one of the things I really wanted was my own plane. Tyler Perry had the exact plane that I wanted, so I reached out to him to get the interior sketches for his plane. I immediately showed the picture to one of my partners. "I'm never flying in a commercial plane domestically ever again," I said.

It may not be your vision to fly privately, but why not create a vision to fly first class? Get out of your comfort zone and treat yourself to a first-class ticket for your next business trip or vacation. Once you experience first class, keep up the work to make that your regular reality. If you don't think any higher of yourself, why should anyone else?

Now, don't get stuck on the airline analogy. If flying privately or first class isn't important to you, that's okay. Your interpretation of first class may be different. First class may simply be achieving the financial wherewithal to take a vacation once a year, especially as you haven't been on a vacation in years. But what about having a first-class vision for your life? What about providing a first-class education for your children? What about creating a first-class business? How about imagining a first-class marriage? First-class appearance? You cannot get to the first-class life if your imagination will allow you to see only visions of coach.

## FIRST-CLASS VISIONING

If first class is important to you in some areas, why not make it important in all areas? Flying first class may not be important to you now, but one day it will be. Once you do enough first-class things, second class doesn't even fit your image anymore. Once you taste first class enough times, second class will never do.

I'm not sitting in the back where they hand out half a Coke and a little pack of peanuts. I don't want to have to buy the sandwiches. I want to be where they are giving out three or four sandwiches. Dick Gregory taught that to me. He said, "Steve, just go see first class. It will condition your mind to settle for nothing less."

First class conditions your mind. Treat yourself every now and then. Go on a nice vacation somewhere. Quit going to your family reunion every year. Drive down to Mississippi to sit under a tree. Dick said to me, "Sometimes you have to take your family somewhere really nice, and watch what happens after that. You'll start dreaming about that real nice place all the time and so will your kids."

## LET YOUR IMAGINATION TAKE OVER FOR YOUR LOGIC

When kids let their imaginations go, they come up with some ideas that are out of this world. Kids don't think about what is logical, practical, or even doable. They just let their imaginations rip. Get back to that space of being like a kid and let your heart and desires guide your vision. There will be time and space for logic down the road. But for now, allow your imagination to take you into that first-class vision that moves you beyond where you are now.

Your vision will matter only when it is connected to your gift. If your vision is disconnected from your purpose, you will be working in opposition to the bigger picture for your life. I am a husband and a father. Those are priorities that are bigger than anything else I do. I can't create a vision that gets in the way of my responsibilities as a husband and a father and think that it will lead me to my best future. Make sure you are clear about what your gift is before you create a vision, because you don't want to be on a first-class flight to the wrong city.

## BELIEVE YOU CAN HAVE IT

God bestowed upon you a gift and placed in you a vision for your gift that does not harm others, because he wants you to have your heart's desire. Do *not* limit your vision because you don't think you are in the right place or know the right people. The greatest thing about creating your vision is that it is as expansive as your imagination. You deserve a first-class future, and your vision should reflect this belief. Even if you had a past filled with failure, you can create a new vision now. Let go of the past and think toward the future. Leave a history of mistakes behind and dream of wonderful, successful tomorrows.

*Success Actions:*
*Write Down Your Vision. Make It Simple and Direct.*

This written expression of your vision for your life is a literal manifestation of the lifestyle you will attain. In writing your vision down, it gains momentum.

_____

_____

_____

_____

_____

_____

## YOUR BOARD WILL MAKE YOU BETTER

I took writing down my dreams further by building a vision board. Not only did I want to read about my vision, I wanted to see my vision. When I first started building my vision board, most people around me didn't understand.

Some people said, "Steve, you have plenty of money; what are you doing with a vision board?" But let me tell you something: I don't rest on my laurels. I want to spend my entire life growing and learning. This may be the case for all successful people I know. Their life is not about getting more; it is about doing more. I have a vision board to offer my life continued direction. There are still things I want to accomplish. I have learned from my past that the best way for me to accomplish my goals is to put them in front of me where I can see them at all times.

Wherever I am—whether I'm sitting at my computer in Atlanta or Chicago or checking my iPhone—the first thing that pops up on all of these screens is my vision board. Regardless of where I am, I want all of my visions to be at the forefront of my mind and in my spirit.

And not only is my vision board visible everywhere I look; every vision I have is directly connected to advancing the areas of my life that are most important to me, and I find ways to make those visions live beyond the screen. Some of the current images on my board include the following:

- **EARNING A 3.5 RATING FOR *THE STEVE HARVEY SHOW*.** I'm at a 1.9 right now; Dr. Phil is at a 3.4 and Ellen DeGeneres is at a 2.9. I've been to both of their houses, and I can tell you that I'm ready for a 3.5 kind of lifestyle.

- **MAKING A DIFFERENCE IN AFRICA.** Right next to my "3.5" is a map of Africa. My goal is to make millions so that I can help millions of people on the continent. I don't know what that looks like yet, but that's the beauty of the vision board. I am open to this vision, and I am talking to people about Africa in ways that I never have before. I am confident that as I keep this vision in front of me, the right opportunity will come along at the right time.

- **PROVIDING SCHOLARSHIPS FOR STUDENTS.** Next to my map of Africa, I have a picture of college students that represents the ten thousand kids who will receive full college scholarships from me and my wife. I plan to give $10 million of my own money to my foundation. I am already on my way to achieving this goal, and the more I focus on it, the more God sends me partners to make this a reality.

I have a few more pictures with my wife, my family, and some major financial goals, but those are personal, and it's important for you to keep some of your visions protected and private for only the people closest to you.

I don't know how I'm going to send ten thousand kids to college or how I will make a difference in Africa or how *The Steve Harvey Show* will reach a 3.5. All I have to do is keep my vision board in front of me and ask, believe, work, and get ready to receive. My vision board helps me to let my imagination go, push every boundary out of the way, and get tuned in to my gift and purpose for being here on Earth.

By using my vision board, I have encouraged others around me to reach their own pinnacles of success. What will you put on your board? Here are some practical tips to help you get started.

## IDENTIFY WHAT YOU WANT TO ACCOMPLISH

Now that you are clear about your vision and your focus, write down five to seven scenarios that represent different areas of your life. Make sure that all of your goals aren't just focused on career and financial gain. Your completed vision should reflect all the areas in your life that are important to you, including family, friends, and relationships; your spiritual, mental, and physical health; being of service; and yes, even those vacations and material things you desire. It's important that you have five to seven visions that reflect several of these areas. This will prevent you from focusing completely on one area of your life while ignoring others. When you look at your completed vision board, it should be a reflection of the whole you.

## DESIGN YOUR BOARD

1. Arrange photos and other images on your board in such a way that it will speak to you and make you want to look at it on a daily basis. You can make it as plain or as elaborate as you want. The key is to make sure that it motivates and inspires you to achieve your dreams. I actually just have pictures and a few words that have great meaning to me. I know others whose boards look like a bedazzled masterpiece. It's all about what works for you.

   Do you want your board to be physical or virtual? This is totally about your lifestyle. If you are like most people, your phone is a lifeline. If that is the case, you should have a digital vision board. That doesn't mean that you don't print it out and place it in your bedroom, office, or even in your car. The beauty of a digital board is that you can have both. If you choose to go old school and simply print pictures and paste them to a piece of paper, the outcome is the same.

2. Pull your pictures or video for your board. As long as the image represents your destination, it will work. Don't be abstract. When you look at this, it should be a clear representation of what you want and where you want to end up.

3. Place the board in as many places as possible. This is important. I know people who have created boards—beautiful vision boards—that they never look at. The point is for you to remind yourself of what you are living and working toward. Don't just let your board gather dust somewhere or become just another screen saver. Make sure you put it where you can see it and keep it in the forefront of your mind. The whole point of having a vision board is for you to create a life worth living.

I truly believe your vision board will help you to lead a better life. Some visions may take longer than others to reach, but if you stay focused and work hard, I am a witness that what you believe will come to pass. There will be some things that you know how to get and other things that you need to leave in God's hands. People of faith often say, Proverbs 3:6, "Acknowledge Him in all your ways, and He will direct your path." When you focus on your vision and connect it to your gift, you are on your way toward success.

# CHAPTER 10

# Man on a Rope

I happen to have had a brief friendship with the late, great Butch Lewis, who was a fight promoter. I didn't spend a lot of time with Butch; most of our conversations were over the phone. But he came to me at a time in my life when I was really, really down. It was around 2005, and I was trying to get my life together. He shared an analogy during one of our conversations that has stuck with me.

I call the analogy "Man on a Rope." For those of us striving to become successful, our journey can be compared to the task of pulling a wagon up a steep hill. Those willing to make the climb are typically business leaders, business owners, heads of families, foundation heads, leaders of children, or pastors of churches. This wagon is like a wooden wagon that you may have seen in Westerns. Our responsibility is to pull that wagon uphill.

This wagon doesn't have rubber wheels on it. It doesn't have a motor. It doesn't have wire spokes. It is just an old wagon that you are pulling up a hill. It has no horse in front of it. It doesn't have a mule in front of it. It has but a single, thick burlap rope. Think of one that can be found in gym class, except twice the size. The rope is very thick and rough; it cuts into the puller's hands—your hands. Yes, you are pulling that wagon up the hill. Your pants are tattered, torn, and dirty. This is a barefoot climb, and you don't have any traction to keep you steady. You are sweating. The rope is over your shoulder, and it is cutting into your skin. It isn't easy.

What makes your journey more challenging is the added weight of the people riding in your wagon. You are carrying them. The only people who can get on the wagon are people whom you allow to board. If you are smart, you will choose based on who will assist you in getting the heavy wagon up the hill. You don't want a cart full of dead weight. No one else can pull the wagon but you. You are the one who wants to become successful. You're the one with the gift and the vision. Whom do you have on your wagon?

People can aid you in your climb, but they can't pull your rope for you. What you are looking for are people who have one leg over the side, pushing with their foot and trying to help you move the wagon up the hill. They are not strong enough on their own to have their own wagon, but they are good enough that you are letting them help you get your wagon up the hill.

You have some people on the wagon whose job it is to cook and bring food to you. Along the way, if you are a man, you may want to find a woman who will get off the wagon to dab your brow, keeping sweat from getting in your eyes. She should be willing to even kick rocks out of the way for you. She will cheer you on.

At night, when you get to sit down and put your foot up against a rock, you can't let go. You have to wrap the rope around your waist when you lean back to take a rest. Everyone else is still on the wagon. Even when you're asleep, your wagon is still heavy. Your wife is allowed to lie with you to give you the strength and the wherewithal so that the next day you are able to continue your journey. But she can't pull the rope. She can inspire you, but she can't pull the rope. She can whisper encouraging words in your ear, but she can't pull the rope for you. That rope is yours and yours alone.

The people in your wagon should play various roles that contribute to your success, or else what is the point of lugging them around? There has to be a person to count your money. There should be someone to provide you with counsel. The problem with dragging everybody up the hill is that some are not contributing. When they see that you are not looking, they lift their foot up and just ride a bit. Some people have gotten so slick with it that they have figured out how to get up in the middle of the wagon and not do anything at all but just ride.

I have watched many successful people's eyes tear up when I have shared this story. It reminds them of the dead weight that they have been carrying and the people who are along for the ride. The friends who have taken advantage of their generosity. And in the worse-case scenario, the spouse or the manager who ran off with their money.

## WHO IS IN YOUR WAGON?

Joel Osteen told me, "God has already lined up all the people in your path to get you to your dreams and your visions; all you have to do is get rid of the wrong ones."

Whom do you have on your wagon who isn't helping you get up the hill? You want people who can propel your vision. When pulling a wagon up a hill, everyone on board must have a role of value or significance. If I have an old wagon and a rope, then I would like to have somebody who at least at night would come down there and put a little fabric softener on the rope to make it a little bit easier. Maybe somebody who has an oil can would grease the wheels. Somebody who has the ability to fix a broken wheel. Someone who does wagon repair in case a rivet comes loose. You want to have people with you who can aid you on your journey.

## ADDING MODELS TO YOUR WAGON

When you start selecting models to put in your wagon, be clear that they are modeling their gift for you. I have seen some terrible choices made when people selected role models to fill the wrong roles. You may select a man who is a brilliant businessman but is an awful husband. Now, as long as he is a business role model, you are in good shape. I recommend you identify role models who provide you guidance and wisdom in your gift, your career, your finances, and your health.

When you choose someone to model, they should have a track record of success. Additionally, the role model should show a commitment to providing direction to others. Mastery in an area doesn't mean you possess energy that should be imitated. You may have access to an elected official who has consistently been reelected, raises tons of money, and actually gets some things done. But if his integrity is off, why would you want to model his actions? Your makeup should guide your selection of role models as much as your gift and goals.

## GETTING RID OF DEAD WEIGHT

Next, let's talk about the kinds of people you do not want on your wagon, because they are dead weight.

You cannot share your dream and vision with everyone. If you are sharing your dreams with people and the first thing they do is try to tell you how your vision won't work, you should immediately disassociate from them. These people don't have vision. They don't have enough insight to think that maybe this isn't right for them, but it is right for you. What you don't need to know is how something won't work; you need to know how it *will* work.

Let go of people who are only around for their personal benefit. Before bonding with someone, I ask myself a couple of questions: Does hiring this person make my enterprise stronger? Does my association with this person make me better? Does this person have information I don't have? Does this individual bring potential income to the table? If he doesn't make me better or stronger, if she doesn't add anything of value, why are we talking? Now, you are going to have a person with a self-serving motive. Effective leaders know that the way to become a great leader is to become an even greater servant. Some people are not even willing to be of service to you, but are coming around you to see what they can get out of you. They see their needs as taking priority over your vision for your future. That's a dangerous person. They can make you feel drained of energy.

Avoid people who are always having a bad day. In their minds, nothing ever works in their favor. They have a chronic "Woe Is Me" campaign that they continue to launch full blast. This kind of negativity depletes enthusiasm. You don't need the woe-is-me speech every day.

Another personality type that I recommend distancing yourself from are those who have to be right all of the time. They go out of their way to be right, but not necessarily correct. Who has time to tangle with this personality? Wherever you are going, this person will not be able to get you there.

You should also be leery of procrastinators. Procrastinators will weigh you down. Action is the prescription for moving forward. Action will eliminate boredom. Procrastinators are waiting, and they often create more excuses to continue waiting: It isn't the right time; I'm going to wait until it's sunny outside; I got up late; I called them and they didn't pick up the phone; they didn't reply to my email. Procrastinators are going nowhere. Do not let them impede your journey to success.

You should be living your life surrounded by people who are like-minded, service-oriented, and grateful, people who are trying to accomplish things, and who bring something to the table.

*Success Actions:*
*Who Has to Go . . . and How?*

Name the people who are currently in your inner circle who have to go—completely—and not simply move to the periphery of your life. How will you make the transition with them individually?

_____

_____

_____

_____

_____

_____

_____

_____

_____

_____

_____

# CHAPTER 11

# There Is No Self-Made Man

I'll be honest with you: Up until just recently, I really believed that I could take on my life by myself. I was raised by two strong parents who taught me that the world doesn't owe me anything. They told me that if I wanted something, I needed to put my head down, lift up a prayer, and get to work. I followed this advice to a tee, and my life was truly a reflection of a "work hard and ask no one for anything" philosophy. For most of my life, this strategy worked.

But I wasn't really winning. I was working twice as hard to get half as much. It wasn't until I humbled myself, started really listening to other successful people and watching how they worked with each other, that I realized there is a different set of rules at play.

I began to recognize and meet people who wanted to help me, who wanted to do business with me, and who actually wanted to see me do well.

I don't want you to deny yourself anything just because you are too proud or stubborn to realize that God often uses other people to assist you in reaching your destiny. These people are like treasure chests waiting at strategic moments in your journey to provide you with what you need. Asking for what you want is the only key you need to open the chest and enjoy the treasure.

Everything we do in life that's worthy of note requires gifts that are beyond our own. How we utilize the blessings of our relationships is the key to making it big.

As you get transfers along your path, you have to connect with others because there is no such thing as a self-made man or woman. No one builds anything of any great magnitude alone. There's nothing wrong with partnering with someone else. Many times people miss out on opportunities because they are trying to keep it all for themselves. Look at it this way—you can either have all of an eight-inch cake or you can have half of a sheet cake. At the end of the day, that half of a sheet cake is much more than having an eight-inch cake all to yourself.

You also have to keep your eyes open for like-minded people, for others who are on the same wavelength as you. Partnerships give you another person to bounce around ideas with, and they can help you see things from an angle that you didn't even consider. Once you find a partner, he or she won't necessarily be your partner for life. Not every-body who begins the journey with you can go where you are headed. When I started out, I had a lot of partners, but I quickly learned that not everyone was capable of going to the next level with me.

## CONNECT WITH OTHER DREAMERS

I am blessed because God kept putting other dreamers in my life to keep fueling me when I couldn't fuel myself. I first learned about connecting to other dreamers at the end of my junior year at Kent State.

Arsenio Hall and I attended Kent State at the same time, and I remember when our whole crew was discuss-ing what we were going to do during the summer. Most of us had jobs lined up for the summer, but Arsenio said, "I'm going to Hollywood." We laughed at him because it didn't make sense to us. I even said, "What are you going to do in Hollywood?" He didn't even flinch, just said, "I'm going to be famous." I saw him taking a few theater classes, but I didn't think he was serious. Sure enough, though, Arsenio went to Hollywood that summer, and I ended up flunking out of school.

After that summer, I forgot about my dreams and started focusing on paying the rent. I was making thirteen dollars an hour at a job I hated, where I worked from midnight to 8 a.m. every day, and came home filthy and exhausted. All of my friends had graduated and started their lives, and there I was working at factory jobs that I could barely keep because of layoffs. I realized that I wasn't living; I was just surviving.

One night a few years later, I was sitting on the edge of the bed, watching TV and preparing to go to work, when I heard ". . . and introducing from Cleveland, Ohio . . . Arsenio Hall." I looked more closely at the television, and sure enough, there was Arsenio on *Don Kirshner's Rock Concert*. Arsenio had done it. There he was telling jokes and becoming a comedian just like he said he would. He made it to Hollywood and he was on his way. I was sitting there in awe, saying, "Wow!" I started calling all of my friends, waking them up, and telling them to turn on their TVs.

When I got to work later that night, I kept saying, "I

know this dude, and he had dreams just like me. If he had a big dream and made it, I could, too." To this day I don't even know if Arsenio knows that he changed my life. But I learned that being around another dreamer can push you when you forget how to dream for yourself.

## ASKING FOR WHAT YOU WANT

There are no self-made men. You need others around you for inspiration and motivation. And I'm certain that at some point you will also need them for material resources or advice. Whatever the case, you need to be bold enough to ask. I didn't always feel this way. In fact, what encouraged me to begin asking was realizing that I had nothing to lose. I also had nothing to prove and nothing to be ashamed of, so rejection was nothing to fear. Recognizing this practically doubled my confidence level. It strengthened me to go forward and ask. You have no idea of the number of successful people around you who are waiting for someone to come up and ask them for assistance or guidance.

I could have saved myself a lot of pain if I didn't mind asking people for things. Little did I know how many people were sitting around just waiting to have a discussion with me, to have an association with me. Magic Johnson doesn't mind sitting down talking. John Hope Bryant doesn't mind talking to me. Tyler Perry doesn't mind talking. The president of the United States doesn't mind talking. Big agencies, such as William Morris Endeavor, don't mind talking to me. The chairman of NBC doesn't mind talking to me. I was so occupied with priding myself on not asking for anything that I almost missed out.

It's okay to sit and brainstorm with like-minded people and share what is going on with you. You may not have to ask for as much as you think. Just the mere fact of your striking up a conversation could be the thing they have been waiting for; maybe this other person is looking for somebody who wants to do something, who is eager to learn, who is eager to share, and that initial conversation will lead to great things. Keep it in perspective; all you need to do is talk to people of like mind, and I promise, they will not mind talking to you.

## IDENTIFY WHAT YOU WANT

How do you expect to get what you need if you don't open up your mouth and ask for it? Our lives are a direct reflection of our communication. If you are unwilling to communicate your needs to your employers, customers, partners, and family members, you can't blame them for not giving you what you need. You don't know everything, you don't know everyone, and you can't do it all alone.

## ALL POWER, NO SHAME

Various research studies illustrate how powerful it is to ask for what we want. Studies show that in most cases people say yes to those people who ask for what they want far more often than people expect. Additionally, most requests seem larger in the requester's head than they are to the requestees. Lesson learned? Asking for what you want gives you a better chance of getting it than not asking. So why don't more of us ask for what we want?

A study done by sociologist Annette Lareau showed how kids from different economic backgrounds view asking questions. Kids from affluent and middle-class environments believed that they were entitled to ask for the things they felt they deserved. They almost willed themselves to have what they wanted by creating a habit and value system of asking for what they want.

On the other side, you have people who grew up like me, in an environment where you were viewed as weak if you didn't know something. And don't even get me started about asking for what you need. So often I didn't do that, because I didn't want anyone to know I needed anything. That was the pride that kept me from getting all that I wanted, needed, and actually deserved. There is no shame in not knowing something, in not having something, or in wanting or needing something. So much of what will determine the difference between a good life and a great life is an ask away. Without shame, you have access to more power.

## BUILDING RELATIONSHIPS

While there is power in the ask, there is also risk involved. People may say no. Some may make assumptions based on our wants or needs, and still others may reject us and our boldness in asking for what we want. But the fear of those responses is increased a thousand times when all of our interactions with people are only transactional.

When you interact with people only when you need or want something, they can see your intentions coming a mile away. Asking for what you want becomes a totally different process when you deal with people based on nurtured relationships. But this can be hard for many of us. We don't want to be vulnerable, and building true relationships requires a higher level of openness. But whether you are attempting to access capital to launch a new business or trying to convince your boss you deserve a raise, a meaningful professional relationship can make all the difference. When people respond to a request, they are usually not just giving a thumbs-up or a thumbs-down to what you asked for. They are actually assessing what they think of you, the risk involved, and the potential return. How do we begin asking for what we want?

Here are six principles to help you get a yes.

1. **KNOW YOUR WORTH.** If you don't know your worth, you are allowing someone else to determine it. But knowing your worth is not enough if you don't communicate it boldly. If you have determined you are worth $150,000 a year, you have to be willing to fight to get as close to that value as possible. In fact, you should be prepared to go in asking for more than $150K to give yourself room to negotiate down to what you want. As with any request, you may not get *exactly* what you want. However, when you know your value and fight for it in a professional way, I

guarantee you will walk away from the table with more than if you had asked for nothing.

2. **RECOGNIZE WHAT YOU DESERVE.** Far too many people—women in particular—put their wants and needs on the back burner, for the benefit of everyone else. There is nothing noble about denying yourself the life you were destined to have to accommodate someone else. That doesn't mean we don't make compromises for people we love or those we are building businesses with. But if your needs are always being put on hold, you have to pause and reprioritize your values and commitments. Warning: Be careful that you don't confuse what you deserve, which is what you work for, with a sense of entitlement, which is what you want but didn't work for.

3. **GET SPECIFIC.** It is important to be specific about what you want and need. Failure to communicate what you need will add frustration and increase your timeline to gaining your success.

4. **DON'T ASSUME ANYTHING.** People are not mind readers. I don't care how well you know someone:

Never assume that they know what you want or need. Even if you think they "should" know, get crystal clear about your needs beforehand.

5. **COMMUNICATE YOUR VALUES.** Be firm about what you will and will not stand for. The quickest route to frustration is a failure to communicate your value system. This can be challenging when you are in a place of real need. But don't be someone who can be easily bought. Don't compromise your standards.

6. **RECOGNIZE THAT "NO" IS *NOT* A REJECTION.** The bank, your boss, and even your significant other will not always say yes. They may not be able to give you what you want. Do the best you can to see the situation from all sides and not just your own before you cut off a relationship, turn down an opportunity, or burn a bridge.

Your gift is waiting for you to fight for what you want. When you build a world that looks the way you want it to, you are giving your gift more room to grow. You have come too far now to talk a good game about what you want without asking for what you want. The worst thing that can happen is someone will say no. The best thing that can happen when you ask for what you want is . . . You Get What You Want and Need.

## Success Actions

List three things you want that you have never asked for:

1. _____

_____

2. _____

_____

3. _____

_____

Why did you not ask for these things?

1. _____

_____

2. _____

_____

3. _____

_____


Identify three people you should ask something of.

1. _____

_____

2. _____

_____

3. _____

_____

# PART THREE

# *Maximizing Your Gift*

# CHAPTER 12

# Tale of the Tape

When I was growing up in Cleveland, I was a boxer. I absolutely loved the sport as a child, and I still love it now. Any true boxing enthusiast can tell you about the Tale of the Tape, which is a prefight analysis that shows detailed measurements for each fighter. When you watch the Tale of the Tape on TV, the measurements typically include each boxer's age, weight, height, and arm reach. Back in the day, it also used to include biceps, chest, waist, thigh, neck, calf, and even ankle measurements. While you and I may not be able to do a whole lot with all those numbers, true fight analysts can identify strengths and weaknesses before a single punch is thrown.

## KNOW YOUR OPPONENT

One of the greatest fights in the history of boxing was the 1974 Rumble in the Jungle, between the undefeated heavyweight champion George Foreman and former heavyweight champion Muhammad Ali. The fight took place in Kinshasa, Zaire (now Democratic Republic of the Congo), and nearly all the experts predicted that the younger, stronger, more powerful champion would defeat the older, flamboyant, but weaker former champion.

Ali knew better than anyone what his strengths and weaknesses were. He knew he couldn't punch harder than Foreman, and he knew that his typical dancing around the ring was not going to have the same impact on Foreman as it had on previous fighters with different skills. Ali assessed his challenger's skills and looked at them next to his own. Using what he learned, he devised a strategy that he had never before tried. For the better part of eight rounds, Ali leaned back against the ropes, allowing Foreman to throw punches that took major effort but caused minimum damage. At other times Ali would get in close to Foreman, lean on him so that Foreman was holding Ali up, and take quick jabs to his face. By the eighth round, Foreman was weak from expending his energy throwing punches as well as from receiving Ali's jabs. Ali knocked Foreman out in that round and stunned many in the boxing world.

Ali was not the stronger fighter on that day. But he was the fighter who had done a better side-by-side assessment of skills. You have to take on this same mind-set as you are looking at new opportunities, new career moves, and even new relationships. Just like in boxing, what is a weakness against one fighter may be a strength against another. When you look at your list of skills, what are your potential advantages and disadvantages?

If you have strong skills in communications, project management, and team building, but you have weaknesses in budgeting and finance, it is unlikely that your skills would match up well for a chief financial officer position. On the flip side, if you have strengths in technology and digital design, your skills could line up well for a chief technology officer. Make sure you know your opportunity, relationship, or job well enough to size up its requirements in relation to your skills so that you can knock it out of the park.

## SUCCESS REQUIRES YOUR BEST EFFORT

You cannot give your best when you don't know what your best is. Knowing your strengths and weaknesses is important because you need to learn how to maximize your wins and minimize your losses. Taking on the challenges of life, business, work, health, and family means you will have to take and throw a lot of punches. Being honest about your weaknesses will put you in a place to take fewer punches and minimize being knocked off your path to success.

Finally, each of us has the ability to either evolve and grow stronger or remain stagnant and become weaker. When you know what you do well, you can develop a strategy for growth. All of this is possible with a little work, but none of it can happen if you don't take the time to know your strengths and acknowledge your weaknesses.

## HOW TO KNOW YOUR
## STRENGTHS AND WEAKNESSES

Assessing your strengths and weaknesses is not an emotional process. Rather, it is a time for cataloging your skills. Knowing what you do well versus what you still need to improve upon will help you to identify your personal skills and traits. As you begin this treasure hunt to uncover your qualities, here are the areas where you may start looking for your strengths and weaknesses.

- **KNOWLEDGE-BASED SKILLS:** These skills include degrees, languages, technical know-how, industry-specific skills, or managerial savvy that you have gained from educational training or professional experience.

- **TRANSFERABLE SKILLS:** These skills include everyday traits that you can bring with you into any situation, such as communication skills, financial knowledge, customer service expertise, leadership aptitude, problem-solving skills, and project management experience.

- **CHARACTER SKILLS:** Traits such as honesty, timeliness, hard work, trustworthiness, and confidence are great characteristics that will serve you well both personally and professionally.

First, let's take a look at your personal and professional relationships. What are the skills you demonstrate in interpersonal relationships? Are you a good listener? Are you supportive? Now think about the areas where there's room for improvement. Can you be more patient? Do you need to work on your ability to compromise?

Next, let's focus on your professional career. What are the skills you have needed to do your job well? What are the skills that your employers ranked you highly on during your performance reviews? What were the areas that were marked for continued growth and improvement?

Now that you have a list of skills in these two major areas, I want you to identify what kind of skill it is (for example, Knowledge-Based, Transferable, or Character). Note whether it is a strength or a weakness, and evaluate each as follows: Superior, Good, Proficient, and Needs Improvement. So that you can get an idea of how to rank your skills, I have included my own Tale of the Tape in the table below.

## STEVE'S PERSONAL TALE OF THE TAPE

| SKILL | TYPE | STRENGTH OR WEAKNESS | RANK |
|---|---|---|---|
| Communications | Transferable | S | Superior |
| Marketing | Knowledge-Based | S | Superior |
| Building International Relationships | Knowledge-Based | W | Needs Improvement |
| Listening | Character | S | Good |
| Budgeting | Transferable | W | Proficient |

This self-assessment will give you an honest picture of yourself. But before you complete your sheet, bear this in mind: You have to complete your assessment based on where you are *today*. No beating yourself up over past weaknesses or undervaluing strengths when you have clearly developed in certain areas.

What are your skills?

## PERSONAL TALE OF THE TAPE

| SKILL | TYPE | STRENGTH OR WEAKNESS | RANK |
|-------|------|----------------------|------|
|       |      |                      |      |
|       |      |                      |      |
|       |      |                      |      |
|       |      |                      |      |
|       |      |                      |      |

## USING AN OUTSIDE OBSERVER

Your personal assessment is important, but you also need an outside perspective. You may want to consider hiring a business-development coach to assess your skills. If that's not possible, you might ask a longtime colleague or a trusted friend to objectively evaluate your skills. If there are a number of people you can rely on in your inner circle, you may want to consider having one person give you a personal assessment and another give you your professional assessment. As you start working with your outside observer, here are three things to keep in mind:

1. **BE OPEN.** Your feedback with your outside observer will be more effective if you can let go of your beliefs and hear what your observer has to say.

2. **KEEP YOUR EMOTIONS IN CHECK.** Your observer may uncover something that could hit a nerve. Don't shut down when you hear something uncomfortable. Stay in the moment and use this conversation as an opportunity to learn and grow.

3. **LISTEN WITH YOUR HEAD AND NOT YOUR HEART.** Identify areas where your strengths and weaknesses impact your life in ways you previously had not thought about.

## MANAGING STRENGTHS
## AND IMPROVING WEAKNESSES

There are traits of your strengths and weaknesses that you must understand to ensure your success.

Stepping Up Your Strengths

- **BE CONFIDENT BUT NOT COCKY.** Know your strengths and use them to your advantage. Be confident enough to insert your skills into opportunities that will provide advancement and growth. However, even your strengths have limits. Know your limitations and manage them well.

- **STAY FIGHT READY.** Floyd Mayweather Jr. is not always the most popular person, but he has the distinction of almost always being at fight weight.

Most boxers have to train for months to get to a fighting weight. Likewise, you have to consistently work on your strengths. Continued education, supplemental training, and reading everything you can get your hands on will not only keep your skills sharp; they will also help you to grow.

- **DEVELOP OR DIE.** If you do not develop other strengths, your enemies will always know what choices you will make. Switch things up, learn and master other skills, and apply them strategically so that you can stay ahead of the marketplace and your industry.

Working on Your Weaknesses

- **PROTECT YOUR WEAKNESSES.** Like Ali, you don't have to expose your weaknesses. Remember to identify opportunities that speak to your strengths.

- **CHOOSE YOUR WEAKNESSES.** Weaknesses are only a detriment if you allow them to be. Create partnerships with people whose strength is your weakness. Learn from them and build that area so that you can grow stronger.

· **DEVELOP OR DIE.** If you stay the same, your enemies will know where to attack you. Continue to develop so that even areas that need improvement can be assets.

Knowing your strengths and weaknesses is without question the difference between your success and your failure. Assess your skills and develop a strategy so that your skills will always be used for your advancement.

## Success Actions

What are the strengths you want to focus on for your next opportunity, job, or relationship?

_____

_____

_____

_____

_____

_____

_____

_____

What are three opportunities you can connect your skills to?

1. _____

_____

2. _____

_____

3. _____

_____

What is one weakness you want to strengthen, and how will you do so?

_____

_____

_____

_____

_____

# CHAPTER 13

# Never Be Afraid
# to Reinvent Yourself

One thing that has helped me throughout my entire career is my total willingness to reinvent myself. When I was the host of *Celebration of Gospel* for thirteen years, that was a complete 180-degree turn from being one of the original Kings of Comedy. I used my past experience of growing up in church to host *Celebration of Gospel*, which then propelled me into a broader space of people.

My willingness to reinvent myself yet again from being a solo act to being part of a touring act with a group of men opened the door for the film *The Original Kings of Comedy*, which then propelled me onto a national level as never before. Next, at the request of HarperCollins, I had an offer to write my first book. I had never set out to become an author, but I released myself from that fear, and the resulting book went on to be a great success. The popularity of *Act Like a Lady, Think Like a Man* led to Fremantle-Media coming to me and saying, "You are very popular among women. We have a game show we'd like you to look at." Thus came the birth of my hosting *Family Feud*.

I always wanted to do a late-night talk show, but after my success with *Family Feud*, NBC and Endemol approached me with, "We have a daytime project for you." I lost my fear of daytime television and launched into doing my own show. My constant willingness to reinvent myself has helped me not to get stuck on stale, meaning desiring one thing my entire life.

Change comes in every person's life. You can either react to it or you can participate in it. I choose to participate in all the changes in my life. If you live your life reacting to change, you are then behind the eight ball. My choice is to be proactive and to participate in the change. I truly believe that that's been a huge part of my success. The more willing you are to accept change and to be a part of change, the more successful you will become.

## MAXIMIZING YOUR EXPERIENCES

Diversifying your gifts also means knowing how to use other experiences in your life. Most of us really only have one talent. My talent is to take information and to immediately transfer it onto other kinds of platforms. I know how to take information and transform it into comedy, inspiration, motivation, or guidance. At one time, I thought my only talent was transforming information into comedy. As I have gotten older, though, my experiences have shown me that I can take that information and transform it in many ways, and by doing so, I become an inspiring, sharing, and motivating person.

If you are a hairdresser, your gifts may lead to teaching or leading seminars at a hair school or creating hair products or hosting your own hair TV show. You never know. You just have to stay open to diversifying your gift.

Let me break it down using my friend Earvin "Magic" Johnson. Magic is one of the greatest basketball players the world has ever seen. But I don't believe that his gift is playing basketball. I believe that his gift is connecting with people in a way that few can. Basketball was a talent. What Magic has done off the court is his gift—strengthening communities with resources and commerce by convincing the right people to believe in his vision. His talent put him in the position of exercising his gift. Watching Magic Johnson navigate a post-basketball career, you realize that this man can talk to anyone, from any background, and make them believe their idea is possible. That is his real gift, and the kinds of business and personal relationships he has been able to create with that gift have far eclipsed his basketball prowess. When you commit yourself to excellence, even a talent can take you to amazing places.

Sinbad was a guy I really looked up to back when I started in comedy. I remember him telling me one evening that he was able to pull in $50,000 per week at some of the clubs where he performed. At the time I thought I was doing all right just making $500 a week, but when I heard about the kind of money that Sinbad could command, I made it my goal to earn that kind of money and then some. My inability to work *all* types of crowds wasn't going to get me any closer to that $50,000 paycheck. I had to step up my game, study my craft, and truly learn what was going on in the world so I could create the kind of jokes that would allow me to share my gift with a broader range of audiences.

You are not a sellout if you expand your gifts and talents for wider appeal among a broader audience or a bigger arena. The more open you are, the faster you will realize your dreams. An expansive vision is necessary when reaching for your life's possibilities. We cannot allow small-mindedness to interfere with our rewards. Step outside your comfort zone and try something new, something adventuresome, when utilizing your gift.

The Bible says, "I've come that they may have life, and have it abundantly." Nowhere in that Scripture does it say, "I've come that you might have a comfortable, safe, boxed-in life that makes everybody happy."

Diversifying your gift presents you with the opportunity to reach people whom you wouldn't have been able to connect with previously. There are windows of blessings that God has just for you if you have the faith to take your gift to the next level.

When I first wrote *Act Like a Lady, Think Like a Man* in 2009, I was diversifying my gift. We have to learn to dream bigger than our past and current circumstances to create a bigger picture that will inspire us to move forward.

## STEEPED BUT NOT STUCK

One group of musicians that I'm really proud of right now is the Roots. If you're not watching the new *Tonight Show*

*Starring Jimmy Fallon*, you are missing out on the chance to see one of the baddest bands in the land do their thing every night. What I love about the Roots is that this is a band that started out as a live hip-hop group in Philadelphia. But when you tune in to *The Tonight Show*, they're playing with *everybody*, from Nas to U2 to Steven Tyler to Willie Nelson. The Roots is a band that is clearly steeped in hip-hop and the traditions of soul music, but these guys are not stuck there. This band clearly appreciates their roots (pun intended), but the band members haven't allowed their past to keep them stuck in one vision for the future of their career.

By all means, I don't want you to throw any of the traditions, legacies, and skills that came along with your gift out of the window. This unique set of traits is what makes your gift different from everyone else's. While you should take the time to accentuate your gift in all the rich techniques and tricks of the trades you have learned over the years, don't get stuck there. I don't want you to fall in the trap of only knowing how to bake a wedding cake the way your mother taught you when you first joined her shop in 1985. I know you play a mean guitar with your band on Saturday night, but don't miss out on the opportunity of learning how to play an acoustic guitar for a retirement party during the week. Who knows? That retirement party might be more live than your Saturday night gig if you pick the right song.

I love the late comedian Richard Pryor. I can probably quote most of the sets from his popular comedy albums, but getting stuck on Pryor is not the kind of comedic skill that would get me invited to host *Celebration of Gospel*. Doing something that makes a church mother laugh is different from rocking a crowd in a comedy club on a Friday night.

When I did my comedy special *Don't Trip . . . He Ain't Through with Me Yet!* in 2006, it was one of the first shows where I played to a predominantly Christian audience. I prayed to God that I wouldn't slip up and cuss in front of these good people. He blessed me with rich, humorous material that was well suited for that audience and beyond. My roots didn't change, just my material.

Don't let your background become a limitation. The smartest folks in business take the best of what they have learned from their parents, mentors, colleagues, and bosses, and use it to build from there. You will never hear an innovator such as Bill Gates, Warren Buffett, or Oprah Winfrey say, "We are doing it this way because that's how it's always been done." Successful people appreciate where they have come from, but they don't let their past set the tone for their future. Successful people are innovators.

## Success Actions

Take a moment to write down all the skills and talents that come along with your gift. It could be as small as knowing how to create an agenda for a meeting or as large as organizing a Labor Day picnic for your office.

_____

_____

_____

_____

_____

_____

_____

_____

List ways that you can diversify or expand your gift to a wider audience or a bigger arena. Don't be afraid to think BIG here. How can you really take your gifts to the next level?

_____

_____

_____

_____

_____

_____

_____

_____

_____

_____

_____

_____

_____

# CHAPTER 14

# The Power of No

Many years ago, I owned a comedy club. One of the things I learned about myself after that business was that I would never, ever sell alcohol to another person. The worst experience I have ever had was talking to drunk people! I told God, when I got out of the comedy club business, I would never promote alcohol again.

It was easy to keep this promise, until Crown Royal became the official sponsor for the Kings of Comedy tour. I was hosting the show when the promoter gave me a list of positive stuff to say about Crown Royal to get people to buy it. I said no. He started telling me how much money we were making because of Crown Royal, which was true. And there is nothing wrong with the product when used in moderation, if that is what you choose to drink. But I had made a promise that I would not use my fame or fortune to promote the consumption of alcohol. I have other vices. I smoke cigars. I'm not perfect, but I do not choose to promote alcohol.

It became a huge problem. The promoter threatened to cut my money and pull the sponsorship. There were a few verbal altercations, along with the promoter standing by the side of the stage trying to make me sell alcohol. This battle went on for about six weeks. He did everything he could think of to make me promote alcoholic beverages. I really liked the people at Crown. They came to the show and were great sponsors. They helped us out in a big way. The Crown on the bag signified the Kings. It was a great tie-in. I explained to Crown Royal that I wouldn't sell the product because I didn't like what it does to people. Who doesn't understand that? Because I am famous, the star of *The Steve Harvey Show*, they realized that if I said it, it would carry a lot more weight. I'm not saying that you are not supposed to drink it. As a person of integrity, I'm saying that I will not sell to people something I won't use.

I had to stand my ground. Crown Royal understood what I was talking about. They understood that they couldn't make me promote their brand. I stood for something. I have always thought it was important to stand for something, and I stood proudly.

"No" is a powerful word. I risked being fired by standing up for what I believed in. Being able to say no will help you become confident in setting personal standards, as well as being comfortable setting boundaries, both of which are critical in your journey toward success.

## THE POWER OF NO

Saying no gives you a set of powers that I like to call "The 5 E's." They are as follows:

**THE POWER OF ENERGY.** Saying no gives you the energy to focus on the things in your life that move you closer to your destiny.

**THE POWER OF REDUCED EGO.** Saying no is also being strong enough to admit that you can't do everything.

Even when we are trying to be the best, we have to realize we are not God. Don't try to do it all. The plan that you have for your gift will guide you.

**THE POWER TO EMPOWER.** Saying no gives you the ability to let someone else shine. Recommend another person for the honor. Your no will open the door for others to rise.

**THE POWER TO END ENABLING.** Some people say yes all the time in order to save other people—to cover for them when they won't step up to the plate. *Stop.* Your no forces someone to step into the place he is being called to. Even if you let him fail once . . . you are helping him in the long run. Your yes is only delaying the inevitable.

**THE POWER TO ROB YOUR ENEMY.** People may want to steal and manipulate your gift. Saying no allows you to use your gift and power in the right place at the right time for the right purpose. Stop giving your gift to those who want to use you for the development of their legacy, at the cost of yours. Do not let anyone distract you from focusing on your vision.

Maximizing this power will help you avoid all kinds of situations that take you further and further off the path to your success.

## THE NO TEST

When I talk to people about saying no, one of the questions I get most often is, "How do you know what to say no to?" And that is a good question. Because not every opportunity, relationship, or experience that comes your way—even if it's something that you want—is good for you. Have you ever thought you wanted something and when you were presented with it, said yes, and shortly after wished you had said no? Me, too. Well, let me give you a list that will help you determine what offers warrant a no.

- Does this opportunity, event, relationship, job, request, etc., move you closer to one or more of the items on your vision board?

    **YES     NO**

- Does this opportunity, event, relationship, job, request, etc., support your gift?

    **YES     NO**

- Does this opportunity, event, relationship, job, request, etc., conflict with a task you are doing—or something that you need to get done—that is in line with one or more of the items on your vision board?

  **YES**     **NO**

- Does this opportunity, event, relationship, job, request, etc., mutually benefit both you and other parties involved (regardless of whom it benefits more)?

  **YES**     **NO**

- Does this opportunity, event, relationship, job, request, etc., conflict with a moral belief, even if it benefits you in other ways?

  **YES**     **NO**

- Are you being fairly compensated (as you see it) for this opportunity, event, relationship, job, request, etc.?

  **YES**     **NO**

Does this help you get closer or take you further from that which you have defined as the goal? Saying no now will reward you with victory later.

# PART FOUR

# Creating
# Your Legacy

# CHAPTER 15

# Healing Your Haters Through Success

The Bible says, "Life and death are in the power of the tongue."

In your quest to become successful and to be more, have more, and enjoy more, there is going to be opposition. Sad to say, but opposition is not always just circumstances; a lot of times it's other people, and those people show up as haters. Every time you make a decision to do more, be more, want more, here comes opposition. The good news is that there is no progress without it. There's no need to address the opposition, because it will be ongoing. The only cure for enemies is success. Your first thought may be, I could really set them straight. Yes, you could. But in order to set them straight, you have to interrupt your climb to do so.

My father told me never to take my foot off a ladder to kick at someone who was kicking at me. When I did that, I would no longer be climbing. While they are kicking, my father told me, I should keep stepping. They can kick only one time. If I continued to climb, they would be left behind. In trying to hurt me, to impede my progress, they would get left behind because they allowed themselves to get sidetracked from their agenda.

Look at success as being on a ladder. Every time you step up one rung on the ladder, you have to lift one foot higher than the other one. If you stop to address a foe, you're not raising your foot to the next level. You're now spending time with a person who is not a decision maker, a power broker, a shaker, or a mover. They are merely a hater. Their one goal is to impede your progress, and the moment you stop to address them, you have helped them accomplish it. You cannot afford to spend a single day engaging with that kind of energy.

No one I know who is serious about business addresses the opposition. They don't have the time. In all of this space, enemies have no significant value anywhere. No advertiser says, "Wait a minute, we're going to advertise here, but let's check what the haters say." No one who prints books says, "Hey, we're about to publish this book, but uh-oh, before we do, let's check and see what the haters are reading." No one who's looking to fill a position says, "Hey, we're looking for haters. We've got a high-paying hater position available." If you understand people of power, decision makers, power brokers, shakers and movers, you know that they don't even know the haters exist. So why should you? My daddy used to always tell me, "Son, don't give 'em a pin to stick you with."

One time I was going through something, and Tyler Perry called me. Tyler said, "Steve, when they blog about you, it's just a blog. If you respond, it's a press conference."

You don't have time for small people. You don't have time for the opposition. Any way you want to look at this, the only way to heal a hater is through success. And at no point in time does it serve you any good to address a hater in any shape, form, or fashion. You are merely putting a spotlight on a dull person. You are giving shine to a person who has no brilliance.

I've learned self-restraint by observing our president. I've never seen a man more noble or regal in the face of adversity. He could stop and address it all, but he doesn't. He just plods along with the job of being the president in the face of intense adversity. We can say the same thing about Nelson Mandela, Martin Luther King Jr., John F. Kennedy, Gandhi, and Mother Teresa.

The Reverend Billy Graham has a wonderful book titled *Nearing Home*. This man dedicated his life to teaching people righteousness and the Word of God. Yet there were still people who criticized him. Throughout history, you can see examples of people who have been attacked. But they just kept putting one foot above the next and continued to climb up to the next rung.

You don't have the time nor can you expend the energy to address opposition. They have no power over you, unless you give it to them. Martin Luther King Jr. said something that I will always remember. He said, "A man can't ride your back unless it's bent." Don't bend over. Stay tall. Keep climbing.

There isn't a week that goes by that someone doesn't have something to say about Steve Harvey. I have no problem standing square in the middle of the public's opinion, because I decided years ago that I would never give anyone the power to define who I am. We live in a free country where people can say whatever they want about me, but at the end of the day, *I* choose—and I'll say that again—*I* choose how those words will affect me and my destiny. And I make the choice every day not to let anyone's negativity stop me from fully operating in my God-given gift.

People who are stuck in the muck and the mire of their misery will spew out their venom on others just to deflect from their own everyday struggles. Some days we can withstand the potshots better than others. The question becomes: How do you stay motivated and moving toward your goals in an environment filled with negativity?

## HOW DOES NEGATIVITY SHOW UP IN OUR LIVES?

On any given day, there is bound to be some kind of negative energy showing up in your life. Whether it's from a coworker, a random person on the street, or, regrettably, your spouse, if you're kicking and breathing, there's sure to be some negativity headed in your direction. Negativity can show up as any pessimistic, critical, or harmful energy that takes you off your path toward success. If you are not careful, not only will that negative energy take you off track, but it will in fact consume you. Before you know it, you'll have spent a whole day thinking, Well, was I really that bad? or, What did they mean by that? So how do we take back our power and stand up tall throughout our journey?

We have to learn to become skilled at deflecting negative energy and keeping our eyes focused on our vision. Look at Oprah. Her vision and ambition to create the OWN Network is a prime example of someone who succeeded despite her naysayers. Her critics were counting her out when she began OWN. You couldn't open a paper or read a blog without someone harping on the network's low ratings or saying, "Who does she think she is to start her own network?" or "She should have just gone on ahead and retired at *The Oprah Winfrey Show*." It's a good thing that Oprah doesn't need anybody's validation to keep her vision moving forward. Oprah went on to do what Oprah does best: She exceeded everyone's expectations by making OWN profitable in less than three years with quality shows such as *Iyanla, Fix My Life,* and Tyler Perry's *The Haves and the Have Nots*. Oprah could easily have taken her billions and gone off to an island somewhere after *The Oprah Winfrey Show*. And to tell you the truth, I wouldn't have been mad at her for doing so. But that woman's drive to win, succeed, and most important, to teach and share with others along the way is truly something to behold.

I remember my first few months hosting *The Steve Harvey Show* on television, when Oprah personally called me. After one of my episodes aired she said, "Steve, don't you let those people talk you out of being who you are. You gotta stay true to *you*." The fact that the Queen of Daytime Television took a moment to call me and help me keep my vision focused and moving in the right direction means more to me than I can ever express.

Take a cue from Oprah's example. You are definitely going to have haters coming from the left, and haters coming from the right. Who are you going to be in the face of your critics? Will you fall under the weight of someone else's opinion? Or will you rise to the occasion and let your haters motivate you to even bigger success?

Here are the four kinds of haters you need to look out for:

## THE "I HATE EVERYTHING" HATER

It could be a beautiful day without a cloud in the sky, and the I Hate Everything Hater will find a reason to complain. Even when good things happen, they never seem to come out of their cloud of contempt. The scary thing about this kind of haters is that they are often angry about something that happened so long ago, they can barely remember the details. The whole world has moved on, but they are stuck in a moment and don't know how to escape. This type of energy can be the worst because it is all-consuming and persistent.

You also have to remember that the energy coming from the I Hate Everything Haters is seldom about you. They don't want to be stuck in their misery any more than you do. But because they can't see their way out, they will lash out at the person closest to them. So if you happen to be in their path, brush their negativity off and get on with your life.

*Stop* giving them a place to store their negativity and they will stop sending it to you. Do you realize how much negative energy we allow people to send to us? Have you ever known someone who tries to find ways to argue with you? They know your buttons, they push them every time, and like clockwork you respond. Don't sit around and take abuse, but rather move and force them to take their negativity somewhere else. I realize that with family and even spouses this can be challenging. But in some relationships we are unfortunately forced to choose between someone else's peace or our own. Don't you dare let their energy destroy your success.

## THE "DRAG YOU DOWN" HATER

The Drag You Down Hater is someone who hates you because they wish they could be you. But instead of doing the things you do to get where you are, they would rather drag you down with them by stealing *your* energy, dreams, and success. The world has done a great job of producing this kind of haters because we have reduced positive messages about people's gifts and increased messages that make people feel entitled to things that are not for them.

Social media has given this enemy a brand-new tool of power. There used to be a time when your haters were just stuck in your physical world. Now on Facebook you can have an enemy in the Midwest who just hates you because you're living a life that they want. While that may seem ridiculous, it speaks to how pervasive this kind of negative energy is. It can come from anyone who is secretly admiring your life but doesn't know how to celebrate you.

In the fall of 2005 I started a new radio contract in New York with syndicated radio in just four markets. People all around me who I thought should have supported me were talking behind my back and saying that I was making a huge mistake. I can't tell you how many folks were laughing at me. But I was determined that I was going to build a radio empire that would fuel the next level of my career. I worked hard, stayed focused, and before I knew it, *The Steve Harvey Morning Show* had expanded into seventy-two markets.

## THE "SITUATIONAL" HATER

Situational Haters are hypocrites who will use you for their own benefit. They are like piranhas in the water, waiting to take you down at any moment. They will compete with you to take advantage of a new opportunity. They will lie and spread misinformation about your character and your performance. These enemies are smart, but the best way to cut them off is to keep your master plans and your ambitions private. If they don't have any information, then they don't have any power over you.

## THE "SELF-HATE" HATER

The Self-Hate Hater is often one of the toughest to defeat because it is the one staring right back at you in the mirror every day. There are times when the negativity that comes from the world is nothing compared to the negative energy we deposit into our own lives. Low self-esteem, doubt, shame, and pessimism have killed more dreams and blocked more success journeys than any outside enemy.

When *you* are your own worst enemy, you have to bring your own light. When you imprison yourself in your own fears, you have to find the keys to set yourself free. In order to get beyond your fears, you have to remember your worth and your value. You have to get up every morning and affirm that talent that God has put inside you. You cannot let your fears, doubts, and insecurities stop you from taking hold of your destiny.

You can navigate the negativity of any of these enemies even if you have never been strong against them before. Become the positive energy that will be a light not just for yourself, but for those around you. Your gift and your vision are relying on it.

# CHAPTER 16

Life's Magical Balance

Gaining life's riches is about more than just earning a paycheck. Being truly wealthy means that you are investing quality time in your marriage or long-term relationship, devoting your time and energy to your children, making your home your sanctuary, and staying on top of your health.

For me, the lights of my world are my wife, Marjorie, our seven children, and working at something I truly love to do. But even beyond those blessings, success is also about truly being in the moment when I am with my family and having the energy and right frame of mind to continue doing the work that I love. Striking the right balance between my family, my career, my home life, and, yes, myself, only happens when I create a place to ensure that each area of my life receives quality attention. Here's how you can begin to truly enjoy and savor the treasures that come along with your gift.

## FALLING OFF BALANCE

There was a time in my career when I truly felt like I was successful. I had the career, the money, the cars, and the clothes. I had finally risen to a level in my comedy career where I could go wherever and buy whatever I wanted. But if I was really honest with myself, I knew I wasn't very happy. I worked hard, and I was proud of my success, but I wasn't always the nicest person to be around. When you don't have all your chips stacked properly, you might get good at hiding the truth from the public, your friends, and even your family. But at the end of the day, you know when your world isn't quite right. I was a successful professional, yet I was missing out on life's true riches. I had an off-the-hook brand with a less-than-stellar biography. I knew I had to create a life system that brought balance to how I looked at all aspects of my world and would prepare me to receive *all* of life's riches instead of just financial riches.

Is your world currently off balance? If so, you're not alone. The demands of today's society almost force you to work a hundred hours per week to become a partner or put in 120 hours just to make it as an entrepreneur. And if you have children, your schedule becomes even more hectic, with homework and after-school programs and weekend activities. Then you have to consider time for exercising, eating right, connecting with your house of worship, and having meaningful time just for you.

I don't believe that a true life balance is about time equity. There will be times when you have to put in more hours at work because your child's tuition depends on the extra income, or when you must put in more time at home because your spouse needs the support. It becomes imperative to find flexible ways to check in with your family when your schedule becomes more demanding, or to negotiate alternative work options with your employer, such as working remotely or working at off-peak hours so that you can be there for your family and still pay the bills. And we all have to find ways to bring our physical well-being closer to the top of our priorities because without our health, we simply cannot function. So, are you ready to create a Success Balance that works for your life?

## THE SUCCESS FORMULA

This is a simple formula that I have taken on in my life, and I want you to find ways to add this into your life, too. Here it is:

HOME + HEALTH + FINANCES = SUCCESS

The beauty of this formula is that as long as you are adding effort to each component every week, you will always maintain a successful balance. There's one catch: Under no circumstances can your priorities for your home, health, or finances ever receive less than 5 percent of your attention each week. Let's dive into each area and explore options for you to invest your time in ways that maximize your gift and position you to receive all life's riches.

## PROTECTING HOME BASE

The word "home" takes on a different meaning for everyone. Your "home" could be the immediate family who lives under your roof, or your "home" could be your close circle of friends who are just like brothers and sisters to you. But whoever gets to reap the benefits of your success, you have to make sure that you are investing the appropriate time and energy into the people who are most important to you. Why? The answer is obvious—by the ways they enrich your life.

We all have our Greatest Hits of Excuses for not spending enough time at home. Here are some of them:

"Baby, you know I'm working these longs hours so that I can make money for *you*!"

"I'm sorry, son, Daddy was just too exhausted to make it to your softball game today."

"I know I promised you that we would catch up for the last two weeks, but this project is *killing me*!"

In the famous words of Billy Dee Williams in the classic 1975 film *Mahogany*: "Success is *nothing* without someone you love to share it with." Our success cannot exist when we don't have the time, space, and energy to share it with our loved ones. Treat your home and family as a SACRED priority, and make sure everyone understands what that means. Make sure that every visitor to your home knows the rules of your house, and respects the place that you call home. Don't allow anyone to just come up in your house and violate the peace and serenity that you have created for you and your family.

Your home is also about creating a space that becomes

your sanctuary. When I got my first significant check, a friend came over to my house and told me I needed to hire a feng shui expert. Now, I'm just a regular country boy from Cleveland, and I certainly didn't know what feng shui was nor was I too keen about having anything called feng up in my house.

But once I learned that feng shui was a technique for aligning your environment with your life's priorities, I was open to it. I invited experts into my home to show me and my wife new color patterns that were supposed to encourage peace and prosperity. They showed us specific ways to arrange the furniture to invite in positive energy and attract wealth. Now, I don't know if all that feng shui really worked (I had my pastor come in and bless the house just in case!), but having every aspect of our space in order made a huge difference in truly making our house a home.

Here are some specific ways to create quality family time:

1. Carve out dedicated family time.

2. Schedule time with your significant other.

3. Create fun time with the kids.

**4.** Pray and stay together.

**5.** Work on your "Honey, do . . ." list.

**6.** Consider hiring help.

## HONORING YOUR HEALTH

I am committed to exercising every day at 3:45 a.m., regardless of whether I am at home or on the road. Why? Because my vision demands it. My daily schedule includes hosting *The Steve Harvey Morning Show* from 6 a.m. to 10 a.m., producing and starring on *The Steve Harvey Show* from 11:30 a.m. to 7:30 p.m., and after that I'm back home to take on my husbandly and fatherly duties. Even if I was ten years younger, there's no way I could manage a demanding schedule such as mine without the *energy* and *endurance* I get from working out.

Here's a typical Steve Harvey schedule:

**3:15 a.m.**    Wake up/prayer

**3:45 a.m.**    Gym workout

| 4:45 a.m. | Report to Steve Harvey Radio Studio |
| --- | --- |
| 5:00 a.m. | Radio show begins |
| 9:00 a.m. | Radio show ends |
| 10:00 a.m. | Conference calls and business updates |
| 10:30 a.m. | Daily talk show production meetings |
| 11:00 a.m. | Hair and makeup/dress |
| 11:30 p.m. | Tape show #1 |
| 2:30 p.m. | Lunch/conversation with Mrs. Harvey; business updates and conference calls |
| 4:45 p.m. | Tape show #2 |
| 6:45 p.m. | Wrap |
| 7:00 p.m. | Postshow production meeting |
| 7:15 p.m. | Depart for home |
| 8:00 p.m. | Resume husband and fatherly duties at home |

At the end of the day, your health is your wealth. We have to put the time in to align our physical, mental, and spiritual well-being. We get one body to do our work here on Earth, so we have to be serious about getting our rest, eating well, and staying fit. Find out what works for you and get about the business of giving your temple the energy it will need to work your gift and fulfill your purpose. If you are slacking on your health, here are a few tips to get you moving in the right direction:

- Make sure you schedule (and keep!) your annual checkups.

- Take the time for some kind of physical activity every day, even if you have to start out with just twenty minutes.

- Choose a healthy diet that will give you the greatest amount of energy and strength for your lifestyle.

- Cut out any excessive alcohol from your diet.

- Drink plenty of water.

I'm not a doctor, but I know that your health is just as much a part of your wealth as the digits in your bank account. Give your body what it needs so that you can have the life you want.

## SURRENDERING TO YOUR SPIRIT

My goal here is not to prescribe a certain belief system or to make you feel guilty about skipping your worship services more often than you attend. But I would encourage you to find a way to surrender to your spirit on a daily basis, whether that's through prayer, meditation, finding a house of worship, or connecting with a small group of like-minded folks. Whatever will help you to remember that there is a bigger picture and a greater purpose for your life, get attuned to that vehicle for your spirit and keep that connection going.

## MONITORING YOUR MENTAL HEALTH

Stress and the pressures of our high-powered lives have the capacity to significantly damage our health and our well-being if we aren't paying attention. If you feel yourself veering into a dangerous emotional place that is beyond talking it out with a friend or a trusted spiritual leader, do not, and I repeat DO NOT, be too proud to check in with a mental health professional. Regardless of your race, gender, or economic status, we can't afford not to take our mental health seriously if we want to fully enjoy our success and peace and happiness with our loved ones.

## GETTING YOUR FINANCIAL HOUSE IN ORDER

Whether you are a recent graduate just starting out or you have multiple businesses with your name on them, we can all be more diligent and proactive about our finances. Those steps can be as small as eating out less often or as big as refinancing your home. Successful people know how to use their money wisely today and set themselves up powerfully for the future.

A few years ago, right after Marjorie and I got married, I got hit with a tax bill to the tune of $20 million. I woke up to the nightmare of discovering that my accountant hadn't filed my taxes in nearly six years. Here I was with the woman of my dreams, and I was facing a financial hole so deep that it was going to take me a minimum of twelve years to climb out of.

I came clean with Marjorie, and I started working hard. I took every speaking engagement, book signing, and in-person appearance I could find. I literally lived at the airport, but I wanted to show my wife that I was serious about getting our financial house in order. After signing a strategic deal to sell the Steve Harvey Radio Network, I was blessed to pay off that bill in half the time. That experience taught me that I never want to have a financial cloud like that hanging over my life ever again.

Financial health is about looking at your entire financial picture. Here are some areas to consider:

- Do you know the difference between good debt (for example, purchasing a home or condo or investing in your child's education) versus bad debt (for example, carrying big balances on high-interest credit cards)?

- What can you do to cut down on your bad debt and increase the payments for your good debt?

- Are you willing to track your spending habits to see where you can cut back?

- Are you putting enough away for your retirement or your child's college fund?

- What can you do to improve your credit score?

- Can you pay off your credit card with the highest interest rate?

· Can you get a lower interest rate on any of your cards?

All of these factors determine how healthy your finances are. Here are five things that every success-oriented person must have for a solid financial foundation.

1. **CREATE A MONTHLY BUDGET.** Developing a budget (and sticking to it!) is essential for creating financial accountability for you and your family.

2. **OPEN A CHECKING AND A SAVINGS ACCOUNT.** Successful people know how to conduct their business aboveboard. Find a bank that you trust and start creating your financial future.

3. **SAVE, SAVE, SAVE.** Whether it's five dollars a week or 10 percent of your paycheck, whatever you can comfortably do, invest in your life and your future by saving NOW.

4. **FILE YOUR TAXES.** It's simple: Pay your taxes each year, on time. Uncle Sam has no regard for your social status. (Just ask any celebrity who thought they could get away with not paying taxes!)

5. **INVEST IN YOUR CHILD'S FINANCIAL LITERACY.** Talk with your children NOW about the importance of budgeting, saving, and investing.

Once you have the basics covered, you can consider the following:

- **HIRING A FINANCIAL PROFESSIONAL.** When you reach that tipping point where you need extra help to file your taxes or diversify your portfolio, it is time to consider hiring a bookkeeper, accountant, or financial planner. If you decide to hire a professional, make sure that you have an open relationship where you can check in about your finances at any time. At the end of the day, it is *your* money!

- **CREATING MULTIPLE INVESTMENT OPPORTUNITIES.** Look into ways to spread out your eggs in multiple baskets.

Remember, your finances, like your health and your home, are only as successful as your investment of time, energy, and excellence make them.

# CHAPTER 17

# God Blesses You
# to Become a Blesser

My mother was a Sunday school teacher. I lost count of the number of lessons she taught me by the time I was twenty years old. At fifty-seven, if I tried to recall them all it would be another book. One of the things she would always say to me was, "God blesses you to become a blesser." Spiritually, I understood that, but let's take it out of the spiritual realm. I want to show you why being a blessing to someone else is one of the most important principles of success.

One of the things I discovered early on is that the more

people you help become successful, the more successful you become. When you share your blessings with someone else, you are fulfilling your purpose in this world as a human being. We are all here to help one another. When you receive a measure of success, on whatever level it is, it's your obligation to teach that or share that with someone else. What I have seen with very successful people is that the more they give, the more God puts them in position to continue to give more. This is a principle that escapes far too many people. It is not enough to have a big house on a hill and not show anyone else how to get a big house on the hill. Then you're up there by yourself and that's no fun.

From the time we were children we had to learn this lesson: You can't play hopscotch by yourself. You can't jump rope by yourself. You can't play hide-and-go-seek by yourself. All the games we played as kids were more fun when shared with others. It's always better when you share the experience with someone else. Don't lose the concept that you learned in childhood now that you are an adult and want to get into the money aspect of your life. Don't lose that simple principle of sharing. Don't stop playing together now.

I love the game of golf, but you can't learn how to play golf and then go out and play it by yourself every day. Golf is a great game where you get to enjoy camaraderie, engage in competition, spend time with family and friends, and enjoy some of the most beautifully landscaped places that you will ever see. That's what makes golf amazing to me. It's better on the course with somebody else in my cart. I can turn to one of my buddies and ask him to take a picture of me. It is important that you share your success and enjoyment with someone in your life. What good is it to see beautiful scenery if there's no one to see it with you? Every great moment in life is better when shared.

When I receive an award and my wife is sitting in the audience, it's so much better because she is there to witness it. When I got my star on the Hollywood Walk of Fame, the best part was that my children were able to share that moment with me. The blessing, too, was that my friends and colleagues were there to celebrate the moment with me. Dr. Phil spoke a few words of congratulations, Ellen gave a speech that was filled with kind words, and Cedric and the entire cast from *The Steve Harvey Show* were there. I got to share this grand moment in my life with the people who matter the most to me.

When you understand that God blesses you to become a blesser, it can open up your life and transform it. The more our creator trusts us, the more He can trust us with.

When I give to someone less fortunate, as much as it can

change their life, it actually does even more for me. When I send a child to school who otherwise couldn't afford to go, God will now put me in a position to receive more resources to send ten more kids to school. Some of you might ask, "Steve, why are you taking your money and sending kids to school?" I would ask you this: "Why do I keep getting the money to send all these kids to school?" When you understand that God blesses you to become a blesser, you will realize that giving back will become an important part of your success.

I don't know if you have noticed, but when rich people get together, they support each other's causes with checks—big checks. The less fortunate may not be able to do that. They sometimes don't support each other's causes on any level, even when they could share in ways that don't involve money. Rich people do because they get it. They view sharing as a fundamental obligation.

What do you think the Met Gala ball is about? All the media shows is the fashion, but the Met Gala is really an event that allows people to give money to a worthy cause, in this case the Metropolitan Museum of Art in New York. It makes people feel good to give back. In big business this principle is called ROI, or return on investment. Successful people understand that giving back ultimately improves their bottom line. Successful people are conditioned to give. When you understand how powerful giving is, you will have more to give.

You don't have to be rich to comprehend this principle. You can start on a smaller level. You can give time at the local food bank. You can spend time helping your aging father with errands. You can volunteer your time at a college fair.

## "TO WHOM MUCH IS GIVEN, MUCH WILL BE REQUIRED"

My mother also taught me, "To whom much is given, much will be required." The requirements are great to those who have been given a lot. As you climb higher, you are going to have to become more of everything. The more you get, the more will be required of you. You have to take more meetings, become more articulate, and be a better manager of time. I don't like reading teleprompters, but now that I am on television, I had to get used to them. I tape too many shows, too many sets, and talk to too many people to remember everything. So I had to learn how to read teleprompters. To whom much is given, much will be required. I had to become more efficient and more proficient.

If you don't adhere to the requirement part, then the giving part stops. Let me be as frank with you as I possibly can: I don't mind taking the time to write this book and compile this information because I realize how blessed I am to be able to do this. I have been beaten up in the process of learning this information. I have taken a lot of hard knocks while learning this information, but it doesn't prevent me from taking the time out of a very busy schedule—as a full-time radio host, a full-time television host, a full-time game show host, a full-time husband, a full-time father, a full-time businessman, and with a full-time touring schedule—to stop and write a book that I hope will benefit others. I have an obligation at this point in my life to educate people and to give them the tools that will help them become more successful. It's now an obligation.

There is no need to get mad at the pastor who has a collection plate circulating when you are sitting there benefiting from the Word and his message. You can't get mad at the bank for making money off your money, because the bank is holding it for you. You can't get mad at the CEO of the United Way because of the large check he gets. He is helping hundreds of millions of people. You can't get mad at the process. Instead, learn from the example. Become one of those people who are willing to share, educate, gift, help, inspire, lead, and push. Afterward, watch to see what comes your way.

People think that the more money you get and hang

on to, the more you will have. In the short view that is true. But eventually the calling is going to come because to whom much is given, much will be required. If you make the money and try to hang on to all of it, God can no longer trust you with the requirement side, so the giving ceases. Just ask anybody who's ever had it all and then lost it. If they are honest with you, they'll attest to this principle.

Success is not just about your ability to achieve, but also your ability to serve through sharing. True success lives in our legacies. If you are able to serve as a model for the next generation, those who grow to greater levels will be as much your legacy as your own accomplishments.

Another key to true success is thankfulness and gratitude. These emotions are demonstrated by sharing with others. Your success shouldn't only be for you; it should also be a blessing for others. I'm talking about really getting to the core of what fuels your gift, what's going to sustain your gift when there are more days in a month than money in your bank account, and what it takes to stand confidently in your vision against all the odds.

By now, you know that your gift is that thing that you do and can do better than nearly anyone else. God isn't going to just open up a door of opportunity for you to use your gift if you're not doing your part to use and share your gift whenever you can. Matthew 25:23 says, "Well done, good and faithful servant! You have been faithful with a few things; I will put you in charge of many things." When you master the "few" you get the "many." When you really love your craft, you don't mind doing it for free or taking the time to mentor someone coming up in the ranks behind you.

You have acknowledged your gift. As you begin to walk in your gift, SUCCESS will begin to follow you wherever you go. Pay it forward.

# ACKNOWLEDGMENTS

If I acknowledged all the people who have helped me get to this point in my life where I'm in a position to write about success, we would run out of paper. Let me just sum it up by saying that I want to thank everyone who has had any hand in any measure of the success that I have attained—you know who you are, and I want to thank you all.

I would like to thank all the people who have played any role and any part. You have been much to me. I want to thank my mentors, even those who have mentored me without even knowing me. I want to thank people who've written catchy and wise sayings. I want to thank you all for that because without you, I don't know that I would be where I am today.

My acknowledgment is to God Almighty, the Creator. It is my belief that God sent all of you my way. Right or wrong, good or bad, positive or negative—you were all placed in the path to create the person that I have become. Although I am an unfinished product, I thank God for who I am and where I am. I thank Him for all of you. I thank Him most of all for His grace and His mercy. I thank Him for His forgiveness. I thank Him because He is not a dream *killer*, but a dream *fulfiller*. I thank Him for all of His guidance, His words, His Scriptures. I thank Him for my life. He is the reason for everything that I am today; He is the backbone of it all.

I would like to thank my children—Brandi, Karli, Morgan, Broderick, Jason, Lori, and Wynton—for providing the constant inspiration for me to be my best for them. I so desperately want to be a man for them to model and admire long after I am gone.

Signed,
An Imperfect Soldier for Christ,
Steve Harvey

**STEVE HARVEY,** the author of the *New York Times* bestsellers *Act Like a Lady, Think Like a Man* and *Straight Talk, No Chaser*, began doing stand-up comedy in the mid-1980s. In 1997 Harvey toured as one of the original Kings of Comedy, along with Cedric "the Entertainer" and Bernie Mac. The comedy act would later be the subject of Spike Lee's feature film *The Original Kings of Comedy*. Steve Harvey is now the host of his syndicated daily talk show and the game show *Family Feud*, in addition to his nationally syndicated *Steve Harvey Morning Show* on the radio. He is also the founder of the Steve and Marjorie Harvey Foundation.